Walking The Walk With God's Kid

DISCLAIMER

The opinions shared in this book are not those of Alcoholics Anonymous. The Twelve-Traditions states; that we of Alcoholic's Anonymous believe that the principle of anonymity has an immense spiritual significance. It reminds us, that we are to place principals before personalities and that we are to practice genuine humility.
The Traditions is the glue that keeps AA together.

*****

I have made a conscious effort to change names and places. It is not my intent to maliciously attack any person or place. I apologize in advance, if what I have written is found to be offensive.

******

If just one, of God's kids finds hope and love in this book.
I would like you to know, that no matter where you are in life or how far down you have gone, you are not alone.

B.J.

To order additional copies, please contact us.
BookSurge, LLC
www.booksurge.com
1-866-308-6235
orders@booksurge.com

Walking The Walk With God's Kid

Barbara Jean

2004

Walking The Walk With God's Kid

CONTENTS

ACKNOWLEDGMENT

To the millions. . .who are friends of Bill Wilson and Doctor Bob. Thank you for being there then and now. The contents of this book have been stolen from your words and example. . .

*****

SPECIAL THANKS

To my family and friends who loved me when I was unlovable

To the folks at BookSurge for your help and patience that has made this book possible

To Cindy Baker-Luna for your love and help
Joane Carroll-Van Nostrand for your love and help

SUMMARY

This a true story of a child who lived on a farm and later moved to a small village in Michigan.

As a child, she was neglected and abused.

She attended school for the first time when she was eight years old.

When she failed the fifth grade, she refused to open any schoolbooks. She was kicked out of school in the ninth grade.

She married at the age of seventeen and had four children when she was twenty-four.

They moved to California where she became a successful real estate broker.

After being in an abusive marriage for fifteen years, she got a divorce.

Soon after, she re-married. She commingled her assets. She was financially raped.

When her husband brought his girlfriend to their home, she trashed her career, family and ran away.

She drank away all her anger, fears, hate and pain until alcohol quit working. When she drank, she could not get drunk.

She had to either get help or die.

Out of desperation, she made a phone call to Alcoholics Anonymous.

She was given a second life and a new way of living sober.

She was married five times before she learned how to have a relationship with herself.

She spent ten years in Colorado Springs where she was able to heal.

She has over twenty-four years of sobriety, "One day at a time."

She is retired and living in Southern California, near the Pacific Ocean.

She has a beautiful relationship with her four adult children and ten grandchildren.

God's Kid has learned to "Walk the Walk" with the help of her Higher Power, She is grateful to AA for her new life.

To All Of God's Kids Who Have Suffered In Silence And Turned Desperation Into Inspiration. To Those Who Are Still Trapped By Fear, May You Find Faith And Freedom. Together "We" Can "Walk The Walk" One Day At A Time With The Help Of A Power Greater Than Ourselves.

To My Many Special Friends Who Held My Hand And Breathed Love, Strength And Hope Into A Broken Soul. Because You Loved Me Unconditionally, I Did Not Walk Alone.

To My Four Adult Children Who Allowed Me To "Walk The Walk And Loved Me When I Was Un-lovable. Thank God You Did Not Trash Me When I Wanted To Trash Myself.

To My Ten Beautiful Grandchildren. I Pray That You Will Gain Wisdom From My Mistakes And Find Your Own Path Without To Many Skinned Knees.

Most Importantly, To God Who Has Given Me Good Orderly Directions.

CHAPTER I

The Abused Child

Barbara was born on October 7th, 1940 at Wayne County General Hospital near Detroit, Michigan. Her mother was forty-two years old with an eighth grade education; she was a full- time mother and housekeeper. Her father was employed as a tool-and-die maker at various machine shops in the area.

Her parents met at Belle Isle near Detroit and they became seriously involved shortly after they met. She had heard that her father was involved with the Purple Gang, a group of Detroit gangsters.

Her mother had been previously married with two children, a son, Jack and a daughter Wanda. She divorced when Jack was six weeks old after discovering that her husband was having an affair.

Out of desperation, her mother sought help from her grandmother who agreed to take the children in at her farm seventy-five miles from Detroit. While in their grandmother's care, Jack developed blood poisoning from a fall on some rusty farm equipment. Because of neglect and gangrene, he had to have his leg amputated.

Wanda was twenty and Jack was eighteen when Barbara was born.

Her father and mother's first child together was a boy, Leonard, who is ten years older than she was. He went to a Military School in Virginia when he was fourteen. A wealthy aunt paid for his education.

Seven years later another boy, Bob, was born who was three years older than Barbara.

Eighteen months after Barbara was born, her mother who was forty-four years old, had a boy, Larry.

Survival was very difficult because of the depression and war. They did not know from one day to the next if they would have enough to eat. Relatives helped when they could. The family would move often in the middle of the night, one-step ahead of the sheriff.

Her father was one of twelve children who settled in Pennsylvania from Sweden. Her grandparents were deceased when she was born. There was very little contact with her father's side of the family. The relatives that she did meet were very cold and unfriendly.

Her mother was mostly German and a native of Detroit.

Her grandfather was placed in an institution after having suffered a stroke.

When she was three years old, they moved out of Detroit to an eighty-acre farm two miles from a very small village.

The old farmhouse they lived in was a shack. They had to prime an outdoor pump for water and carry it inside. They cooked on an old coal stove. Water had to be heated so they could take a bath once a week.

The house was located on a small hill overlooking a dirt road. There were a couple sheds and an outhouse and a collapsed barn that had been struck by a tornado.

Barbara's mother had ongoing nervous breakdowns and depression. She would threatened to run away or lay down on the railroad tracks. She spoke often of ending her life. Her brother, Bob was primarily responsible for watching over Barbara. He was very vocal about how much he hated his sister.

The farm was isolated; they grew up with very little outside contacts. Occasionally the kids would go to the village.

A friendly old man who would walk past the farmhouse, offer the kids apples. Bob told her not to eat the apples because they were poisoned. After that, Barbara hid whenever she saw the man.

One day, her mother arranged for a neighbor girl to visit. Seeing how pretty and well dressed the girl was, she wanted her to leave.

Barbara was embarrassed about how she looked; wearing clothes that had been made from feed sacks, shoes that were falling apart and her hair full of snarls.

She started school shortly before her fifth birthday. When she started school, she would have to walk two miles.

Bob was responsible for walking Barbara to school. This was the beginning of many scary and abusive trips into the village.

Bob would take a short cut along the train tracks and told her that the trains were going to suck her in under the wheels. Then he would run ahead leaving her hanging onto a fence, crying. There were times when he would cut through fields of snow leaving Barbara behind. She thought that she was going to freeze to death after being stuck in the snowdrifts.

There were many days that Barbara went hungry because Bob had eaten her packed lunch. She attended kindergarten for less than a month. Her mother taught her the three R's at home.

*****

At the age of five, Barbara learned to hate. She did not trust anyone. She had experienced loneliness, betrayal, abuse and anger.

Bob enjoyed seeing his sister in pain; he would torture her with twisting and bending of her fingers or arms. Whenever he was nice to her, there was always a price to pay. Barbara was helpless and did not have anyone who she could turn to for help. She was defenseless!

She would look for treasures at the old city dump near where she lived. Bob told her that there was quick sand in the dump.

She believed the lies of her older brother, who controlled her with fear.

*****

Her mother was emotionally dead inside and unable to show any kind of affection or love. The only love that she knew came from an old barn cat and her teddy bear. The cat got ran over by a car and her teddy bear disappeared. She later learned that Bob had buried her bear under an apple tree.

She would hide in the old barn and suck her thumb. She was severely disciplined when she was caught sucking her thumb. Her mother made several cruel attempts to break her from the filthy habit. She put chicken shit on her fingers, tied her to a bed and beat her hands.

Barbara was constantly on guard when Bob was around. He would include his friends in his sick games. If he failed at his latest plot or if she escaped, he would try harder at his next attempt.

Her father's work ended in the city. He opened a gun shop in the village. He would repair and sell guns to the people in the area. She was not allowed in the shop but managed to sneak a peek into the back door a couple times. Her father would bring strangers to the farm and they would target practice and drink beer.

On one occasion, she wanted to see what they were doing. Her father had her hold a gun and shoot at a beer bottle. She was knocked to the ground and quickly lost interest in what they were doing. She learned to respect and to fear guns.

Her mother learned to drive when she was forty-five years old. They would visit her grandmother's farm about twenty-five miles from where they lived. Being at her grandmothers and with her cousins was the highlight of her young life. Her grandmother would kill a couple chickens that roamed the yard for dinner. The cousins would look for mischief or wait outside for the dinner bell to ring. The adults prepared food on a coal stove and the men sat in the yard under a huge pine tree drinking beer.

Barbara's father was seldom home, leaving her Mother alone most of the time with the children. Her mother tried to make the best of what little they had. They ate chicken that was raised on the farm and vegetables from their garden. Her mother made soap and did a lot of canning. Very few items were purchased from the stores. Life was very simple, but for her mother it was pure hell.

Her half sister, Wanda, graduated from college and secured a position with the Detroit school district. She helped the family whenever she could. Her visits were rare and very special. The girl looked at her older sister with admiration and wonder.

One afternoon the girl's mother went to visit her grandmother. When they got there, her mother sent her ahead to see if her grandmother was home. She found her in the basement on the floor where she had been gathering coal. She ran to her mother for help. She learned later that her grandmother had had a stroke. She died shortly after.

The farm was sold when Barbara was eight years old. Her father bought a home in the next village about ten miles away.

Her mother reassured her that the quality of their lives would improve. She had mixed feelings about moving to a new area.

*****

The house that they bought was an old barn that had been converted. It was obvious when she saw the opening upstairs where hay was tossed down. She was disappointed when she saw the ugly house. It was without running water, no indoor plumbing, and a dirty gray. It was in worse condition than the farmhouse that she had lived in previously. She was angry about having been lied to. She was reassured that the house was going to be fixed up.

Neighbor kids watched the new family move in from the sidewalk. Barbara was forced to go outside to meet them. As she stood in front of them, she did not know what to do or say. She wanted to run and hide, but did not have any place to run too.

As much as she wanted and needed friends, she was lacking in social skills.

*****

Her half-brother, Jack, would make an occasional surprise visit. He would play his guitar, sing and tell stories. He spoke about jumping freight trains and traveled all over the U.S. The girl enjoyed his stories even if she did not believe him.

She was fascinated with how well he got around with one leg and crutches. He would tell people that he lost his leg in the war. She would challenge him to races that he always won.

Leonard attended the University of Virginia and Michigan State. His major was journalism. He became proficient in Spanish due to his association with some Cuban's at the University.

When Leonard did come home on breaks, he was very quiet and reserved. He would leave money around knowing his sister was a thief. When he caught her, he would have her take off her shoes where she had hidden the money.

Bob made friends easily and it did not take long before he had his own little gang. As he got older, he became more aggressive and demanding. The girl was forced on many occasions to submit to his demands. She had to beg for relief before he would stop his torture. He would blackmail her into stealing for him. She was forced to comply or suffer the consequences.

Bob, with the help of his friends, spread ugly rumors about his sister. Guilty or not, it did not take long before she was unjustly labeled.

At eleven years old, she wanted to die. The hurt and hate was so strong. She was afraid to be home alone without protection.

Larry, the youngest brother was sheltered from the family conflicts. He spent his summers with an aunt and uncle in Pennsylvania. He was out of the war zone

*****

Barbara's mother found religion at the local Baptist Church and this became her salvation. She mellowed out and appeared to be much happier. She was very dedicated and active with the church. There were times when the girl would wash dishes and sing gospel songs with her mother. For six years after her mother joined the church, the girl attended without missing a Sunday.

Their life was centered around the church, attending Bible studies and prayer meetings. She learned about how God knew everything about you, even your thoughts. She learned about how bad we were and that the devil was out to get us. This looked like a no win situation!

She was convinced that she was in big trouble, adding guilt and religious fear to an already confused mind.

In rebellion, she used her mouth to alienate and shock people from the church with profanity. She was saved three times. Nothing changed and she was convinced that God did not want her.

The church was very strict with what they could or could not do; if it was fun, it was not allowed. She began to question the conflicting messages. What she read, what she saw, and what she heard, did not match up.

She concluded that if she was going to burn in hell, she might as well have fun getting there. At the age of fourteen, she decided to escape the religious propaganda.

*****

Her father closed his gun shop and went to work for one of the area's job shops. She would sit on the curb on Friday nights waiting for him to come home, so she could collect her allowance. She would usually buy candy and share it with the neighbor kids. As long as she had candy, she had friends.

The home got new siding that covered the ugly gray. For the first time they had a real bathroom with hot and cold running water and a tub. Wanda bought their mother an electric stove and relatives gave them some furniture. Her Mother tried to make it nice by adding her special touches.

Sunday's was family day and in the afternoon, they usually had their best meal of the week together. The table was set with the good dishes and linens. The children were expected to use their best manners, and if they got out of line, they would be hit on the back of the hand with the handle of a knife.

Meal times together were usually tense. Inevitably, a conflict would arise between Bob and her father. On one occasion, Bob pulled the tablecloth off and everything went flying. When the table exploded, whoever remained seated ate in silence. Her father would usually leave before he had finished eating. The girl does not remember a time when they were all together without some conflict.

Barbara did not see much of her father; he came home to bathe and change clothes. It could be days, weeks or months before he was seen again. It was common knowledge that he was either at the beer joints or with a woman. She would look for him at the taverns in town. She was concerned about his not being home. Occasionally she got lucky and found him.

She wanted to be with her father and begged him to take her with him. They would travel up and down old Grand River, stopping at one of six taverns. She was fed junk food and sodas.

She was fourteen years old before she had her own room, prior to that she slept with her mother. Her father and Bob shared a room together upstairs. This seemed like a strange sleeping arrangement. Her mother said that she refused to sleep with her father because he wet the bed.

When her father was home any length of time, he would get a report about what the kids were doing or not doing. Good or bad, she could expect to be punished for something that was long forgotten. If she hid or ran when he was home, he would come into her room late at night flipping the light switch on and off. If she did not respond, he would shake her bed, yelling and swearing.

*****

Barbara's first real day of school was when she was eight years old and in the second grade. Without any previous schooling, she was terrified.

Seeing so many kids together was very intimidating. She

was unable to communicate without using profanity. She stayed away from the groups and became an observer.

Fear interfered with her ability to learn. She lacked confidence and was constantly being teased by the kids. She was not competitive and preferred to watch from a distance.

She was held back in the fifth grade because of her problems with comprehension. This was devastating to her. If you were held back, you were labeled as being dumb or stupid.

After that, she did not open or own a schoolbook. She was constantly in trouble or being disciplined by the teachers. She was taken outside of the classroom by one teacher and beaten with a millimeter bar.

Another time, she was asked who won the Kentucky Derby in 1938. Her response was, "How in the hell should I know?" She was kicked out of class and told to write "Lincoln's Gettysburg" address fifty times.

Another time she had to write a 10,000-word theme on the Civil War. When she handed it to the principal, she asked, "By the way, who won?"

She did a lot of I will not's. She developed beautiful penmanship with all her writing assignments.

She began to plot her escape from school. She knew that if she had money, she could buy what she needed, friends and acceptance. What she really needed was a job. She stole what she could get her hands on until she was banned from the stores.

Home was not a place where she could bring friends. She took to the streets and found a new home at the local pool hall. The owners were good to her; she adopted them as her Ma and Pop.

She walked over to the wild side.

She did not give a damn about anyone. She would flip people off as a show of her defiance. She would smoke in public and used profanity as if it was her second language.

She tried to act and talk tough. She looked for someone who could rescue her and take her away.

The friends that she had were from similar dysfunctional single-parent homes.

She had a few babysitting jobs and did what she could to find work. She worked from 4:00 p.m. to midnight at a truck stop, washing dishes for twenty-five cents an hour.

She was able to buy herself some badly needed clothes with the money that she made. From that day on, she was responsible for buying all of her clothes. She had an account with a local dry goods store and paid them back, one dollar at a time.

She managed to drag herself to school and slept through most of her classes. She was called into the principal's office and told that she was wasting the taxpayer's money. He suggested that she quit. She walked out from the ninth grade.

*****

The boys would circle the block where she lived, honking their horns wanting her to come out to play. If this happened when her dad was home, he would go berserk. Her mother would run to the neighbors to listen in on the party line when she got a phone call.

She was not interested in boys. She was interested in what they could do for her. She was especially interested in one boy who owned a car. On occasion, they would go to the lake to party. She would not let anyone get to close to her; she just watched.

Her mother got upset with her when she learned about her going to the pool hall. She would come after her, dragging her out by the hair, kicking and screaming. As soon as she could escape, she would return.

She accepted the labels that had been given to her. It was

amazing how small-town gossip can blow things up and makes them sound worse than they really were. What they saw her doing reinforced the gossip.

When home, she would retreat to her room where she had a radio that brought in two stations, baseball and classical music.

*****

She finally succeeded in keeping Bob out of her room. She could not take anymore of his abuse and she threatened to kill him if he ever tried to touch her again. He knew that she was serious. Fear became his shadow once his actions became known.

Bob offered to pay $5.00 to anyone who could get into her pants.

Barbara was scared from cigarette burns and being cut and fingers that were broken by Bob.

The fighting continued in the house with Bob and her Dad. One night, someone upstairs lit a cherry bomb. Her mother panicked and called the police. She thought that someone had been shot. When the police arrived, they confiscated twenty-three guns including Larry's BB gun. In addition, they took all ammunition, sabers and swords.

Soon after, Bob was kicked out of high school. He got a room and moved a couple towns away where he attended a new school. At night, he would operate the movie projectors for the local theater.

Her first crush was with a local farm boy. He took her places and spent money on her. He was caring and listened to her sob stories.

Weekends and days, when she had time, she would work at her mother's Laundromat. She washed, folded and ironed clothes for the local people. This kept her close to her mother's watchful eye.

When she was not working, she would attend parties wherever and whenever friends were meeting. The first drink that she had was Mogen-David wine. She got sick and had no further interest in drinking. Boys tolerated her and stayed away.

Her mother was very strict about curfews and would set her alarm clock for the time that she was due home. If she were not home when the alarm went off, her mother would be waiting for her on the front porch.

At sixteen she fell in love and was the happiest, that she had ever been in her life. Dennis came from a good family; he was attractive and treated her with kindness. She wanted this relationship to last a lifetime.

He had graduated from high school and enlisted in the Air Force. She agreed to wait forever for him. While he was at basic training, they kept close contact by mail.

When he came home on leave, they got together. He was the first boy that she had been with sexually. After that, everything changed and he refused to have anything to do with her.

He probably collected the $5.00 from her brother.

CHAPTER 2

The Abused Wife

Barbara was walking home after having worked at her mother's Laundromat when she heard a loud wolf whistle. A car pulled up with a Japanese American named Ben. He asked if she was going to a birthday party that night.

She did not know about the party and had made other plans. Once home, she had second thoughts and decided to go. There was a person who she was especially interested in seeing. She had hoped that he would be there.

When she arrived, she saw him and told him know that she was interested in him. He was polite and said that she was a nice girl but, too young, she was seventeen. Disappointed she sat on a couch unsure of what she wanted to do next.

Soon after Ben arrived and came over to where she was sitting. He asked her if she would like something to drink, she replied "anything." He returned with a drink of whiskey and coke. She drank it as if it was soda pop. After a couple drinks, her head started to spin. She went outside, with Ben following. Once she hit the cold night air, she got sick and passed out.

Ben had her get into his car and took her to a farmer's field. He laid out a blanket for her to lie down on and tried to get fresh. She still had presence of mind to know what was going on and protested against his advancements.

Ben took her home and she crawled up the stairs to her room. She had never been that sick in her life!

A couple days later Ben called to ask how she was. He wanted to take her to the drive-inn movie the next night. He picked her up in his old Dodge coupe and stopped for a six-pack of beer on the way. She had to fight him off from putting his hands on the wrong places. She tried to make it clearly understood that she was only interested in being a friend. He completely ignored her request and continued to be aggressive. He finally took her home.

He called and asked her out again after promising to be good. He gave her double messages, one of indifference and another of kindness. He was friendly, yet unfriendly! He was twenty-four years old, seven years older than she was. He had just finished serving two years in the Army. She had no romantic interest in him and was uncomfortable with their racial differences.

Barbara continued to see Ben, just for something to do. One evening when he picked her up, she noticed that he was acting strangely. He became extremely aggressive and determined to have sex. She was not strong enough to stop him. He date raped her!

When she was home safely in her bed, she was overcome with emotions. She felt it was her fault for continuing to see him, thinking that he could be a friend.

She was confused and felt obligated to continue the relationship.

She quit fighting him when he forced himself on her. She gave in to his cruelty and insensitivity.

*****

She thought she was pregnant and called Ben. He encouraged her to see a doctor who confirmed that she was pregnant.

When she told Ben what the results were, he went into a

rage accusing her of ruining his life. It was entirely her fault as far as he was concerned.

She tried to find a solution but there was none other than giving the child up for adoption. She was seventeen and definitely not ready for marriage, especially to this man.

It was several days before Ben got back in contact with her. His only comment was that they would have to get married.

She told her mother what was up and she agreed to have a statement notarized giving her permission for them to get married. When her father found out, he went to his favorite tavern and told his friends that a Jap had knocked up his daughter. To his surprise, someone who knew Ben spoke out in his defense.

On November 23, 1957, they went to Angola, Indiana to get married. They took a couple of Ben's friends. They made nasty remarks and insults to her while they were on the road.

Ben had made it clear, that she was going to pay for messing up his life. She thought that since she had made her bed, she was going to have to lay in it. They were not very happy when they went to the preacher and said their, "I do's."

In her own way, she made a promise to God that she would be a good wife and mother.

Ben stayed drunk for three days and was verbally, physically, mentally and sexually abusive. She was kept awake all night with one assault after another, crying for mercy. She was told that she was like a horse and needed to have her spirits broken.

She was told what her wifely responsibilities were to be. Her first obligation was to take care of Ben's needs. She was to spread her legs at his demand. She felt like a vagina!

*****

They rented a small, furnished apartment and set up housekeeping. She did not have a clue what to do for Ben or how. She had never taken care of anyone, and his needs were very demanding. Whenever she did anything that displeased him, she would catch holy hell. He would yell or threaten her if he was upset. She was careful not to repeat the same mistake twice.

He would become outraged if she asked him for help. He would defiantly refuse, saying that it was not his job. She was told to shut up and to speak only when he spoke to her. She was afraid to say anything around him. There was very little communication and her days were lonely.

In many ways, her abusive marriage was similar to what she had experienced around her brother.

She moved some heavy furniture and did a lot of lifting in their new apartment. One late night, she had severe stomach pain. It felt like a knife or razor was cutting at her stomach. She went to the bathroom and noticed that she was bleeding. She tried to wake Ben for help but he turned away and ignored her. That night she had a miscarriage.

Afterwards, her first thoughts were about getting out of this awful marriage. She told Ben that she wanted a divorce, he said, "no." He told her to get a job. She was trapped; there was no one or nowhere that she could go to for help.

She got pregnant again shortly after the miscarriage. Ben told her not to depend on him to help with a child.

When Ben was not working, he was out hunting or fishing.

*****

She was not given any special consideration during her pregnancy. She looked forward to having a baby who she could love. Having this child meant the world to her.

Ben was even more sexually abusive and demanding as her due date got closer. If she complained, he became more forceful.

He insisted on having sex when she was in labor and on the day that she came home from the hospital.

She had thirty-six-hours of labor. Ben got upset with her for taking so long to deliver. On January 25, 1959 her son, Joel was born. She was so happy when she saw how perfect he was. She was amazed by the miracle of giving birth. Her heart was filled with joy when she held her son.

Joel was a happy contented little boy. Her lonely days were filled with love. Ben was jealous the time that she spent doting over the baby.

The physical abuse started again when Joel was about six weeks old. She was not responding fast enough to Ben's demands. She stood up to him for the first time and told him that if he continued, she would take the baby and leave.

She was serious and determined to find a way out. The physical abuse stopped. The sexual abuse increased.

She loved being a mother and took a lot of pride when Joel got his first tooth, gave his first smile, cooed, crawled and learned to walk. Every little thing that he did made her happy. He was so special to her; he gave her life a purpose. She dreamed of all the things that she wanted for him.

*****

Ben stayed away from home when he was not working afternoons. It was a relief not to have him around. When he was home, he was in another world. He was completely unattached and took no interest in his family.

Ben could be very subtle when he inflicted his abuse. She was completely invalidated in every area and reduced to being a slave. She believed his bullshit and questioned herself. She took the blame for everything. She tried harder to be a better housekeeper, wife, and mother.

When Ben was upset, he would respond by getting in her face with his fist, yelling.

Ben was a supervisor over eighteen women and believed to get results; he had to come down on them. He carried this philosophy into his personal life. Barbara was his employee.

*****

She loved being a mother and wanted more children.

She was at the fair when she went into labor for their second child. On August I, 1960, she gave birth to a girl, Jan., another miracle.

Joel was eighteen months old when his sister was born.

She was grateful that her labor and delivery time was short.

Ben was not enthused or sensitive about being a father again.

Barbara's days were busy with the babies. She encouraged Joel to love his sister and to be good to her. He was attentive and accepting of her and did not show any indications of being jealous.

*****

Barbara inherited her aunt's wardrobe and $1,000. For the first time in her life, she had a closet full of beautiful clothes. She was able to make a down payment on a better home in the country.

Her father gave her a lot in town that she sold. She was able to buy some badly needed appliances for her home.

She was happy about having a good place for her children to be raised.

Barbara had a friend who lent her books and encouraged her to read. She struggled to pronounce the words and had difficulty with comprehension. The more she read the more she was able to absorb. Her friends would ask her about what she had read; she would give them a book report.

This was the beginning of her escape into books. Her mind opened up to a completely new way of thinking

*****

Barbara worked part time at a county elementary school where she watched the children while they were on recess and lunch breaks.

When school was out she would sweep the classrooms and clean the bathrooms.

While working at the school she got hepatitis and became very ill. Ben refused to help her and told her that being sick was all in her head. She did not have the privilege of being sick.

She was expecting her third child and needed help. She asked her cousin, who was in between jobs, if she could to help her; she agreed.

When she went into labor, she had to be quarantined in the hospital. Her labor was long and hard. Ben was very uncomfortable being in the same room with her.

When the baby finally arrived, Ben announced that it was a boy. The doctor corrected him and told him that it was a girl. He got upset and left the hospital. She did not see him until it was time for her and the baby to go home.

On May 22, 1962 their third child, Susan, was born.

There was something special about Susan. Unlike the others, she loved being held and rocked. She would scoot, pulling herself by the arms, dragging her legs. Her grunts or pointing would assure her that she could get what she wanted.

Susan was content playing alone with her dolls while the older two ran around the house.

Barbara became concerned about Susan and had her checked out by a pediatrician. They were not able to find anything wrong with her. Barbara had to exercise her leg muscles and ignored her. Soon after, she was on her feet, walking around furniture.

*****

Ben continued to work afternoons and was home long enough to stir up the kids with his teasing. Barbara had very little communication and absolutely no affection from him.

If they did go out together socially she was afraid to mix or talk to anyone. She would watch Ben getting drunk. She knew that when they got home it was going to be a night of hell.

Whenever she confronted him, he would explode and go into a rage.

Barbara was expected to get up at 2:00 a.m. when Ben got home from work to fix his breakfast. She would have to shovel coal in the furnace and take care of the baby's night feedings.

Ben's responsibility began and ended with the paycheck.

She was constantly being told that she was a leach.

She shared babysitting with friends so she could go to the store or doctors.

When they did go out together, she would always drive. Ben's deliberate reckless driving scared her; she got upset, especially when the kids were in the car. Out of her concerns for her children's safety and self-preservation, she insisted on driving.

She was once asked if it was a Japanese custom for the wife to drive.

*****

Her last and third daughter, Becky, was born July 31, 1964. This baby was very fussy and had problems with formula...

Becky loved men. If there were a room with ten women and one man, she would go to the man and want to be held. When she took Becky to the store, every man that she saw, she would call Daddy.

Barbara had diapers and bottles for over eight years. There were days when it was hard balancing her time with four small children.

She would collapse at the end of the day and did not dare to complain. She was told that if she wanted children, she could take care of them.

*****

Joel had a bad kidney infection and had to be hospitalized. When his infection returned, she insisted on seeing a doctor at the University Hospital. After being checked over, it was determined that he needed immediate surgery. After surgery, she was told that he had kidney damage.

*****

She suffered in silence, dying inside.

She began attending the Lutheran Church and took the children with her. She looked forward to Sundays and attending church. She got strength when she had something to believe in. All four of the children were baptized on a Palm Sunday.

Ben started to give her a hard time about going to church. He called her a religious fanatic. To keep the peace she quit going to church.

*****

On occasional weekends, they would play cards with another couple. Ben was always pleasant and attentive toward her girlfriend. After the company went home, he reverted to being abusive.

After nine years of marriage, they took their first family vacation together.

Barbara managed to save some money so they could go to California where Ben had family. They rented a tent trailer and hired a babysitter to travel with them. Ben told her that he was not going to help drive, he was going along for the ride.

Barbara was excited about getting away from Michigan. She drove 90% of the 5,000 miles that they traveled. Ben ignored her except when he wanted something.

When they returned home, she was exhausted and had regrets about the trip.

*****

One day she found her daughter, Jan, playing alone outside of the school. The teacher said that she would let Jan do whatever she wanted. Jan was so adorable and sweet, she could charm her teacher. When she went into the first grade, she did not like school. She had a hard time sitting still and focusing.

Some of the neighbor kids started making racial remarks to her kids. Barbara was a very protective mother and took offense at the comments. She had not thought about the children's interracial background until the name-calling started.

*****

Ben would sometimes stay out all night. She did not dare to question his activities. She did not care what he was doing.

There was a time when Ben questioned and accused her of infidelity.

Ben's brother and one of his friends would stop by in the evenings to visit. She thought that they were too friendly. She suspected that Ben was trying to set her up.

She spoke to him about the visits and soon after, they stopped.

The company that Ben was working for was letting some people go. It was just a matter of time before they would shut down.

Barbara suggested that they sell the house and move to California. To her surprise, Ben agreed, if they could get a good price for the house.

Barbara placed an advertisement in a large local newspaper and within a week, the house was sold.

Ben loaded up a U-Haul with their few possessions and took off for California with his dog. He could not leave fast enough and did not say good-by.

*****

Barbara and the children went to her mothers to wait for word from Ben that arrangements had been made for them to join him.

Barbara was twenty-five years old with four small children.

She waited a couple of weeks for Ben to call; she did not hear anything from him. She reassured her children that this was a temporary arrangement until they could join their father.

She tried to be considerate and appreciative to her mother, fully aware of how they had imposed upon her.

There were days when it was hard to keep four spirited, active children under control.

When she looked around the old family home, she could see the busted doors and scars from past wars. She was reminded of how desperate she was to get out and be on her own.

A couple more weeks went by and Barbara had not heard from Ben. It became apparent that her mother was having a hard time coping. The children were acting up and missing their dad. It was obvious that her mother was getting anxious for them to leave.

Her mother began talking to Barbara about being abandoned and encouraged her to check up on Ben. Winter was approaching and she knew that it would not be long before traveling in the mountains could be dangerous.

She felt an urgency to get on the road.

Ben's niece was getting married the next week. She knew that she could find him at his sister's that weekend.

Barbara packed the car and hit the road for California, to find Ben. She had a supply of diet pills and every time she gassed up, she will take a pill. When they arrived at the California State line, she was exhausted.

She got a motel room where she collapsed from fatigue. The children were telling people that they were going to California to find their dad. They did not realize that they were already in California.

After getting some good rest, they continued to the Fresno area. She got a motel room and they went on a search for Ben. The kids were excited about surprising their dad.

They found Ben at the church where they were having the wedding rehearsal. The children were happy to see their dad and ran up to him. When Ben saw the children, he went into a rage. He screamed and threatened, saying that he did not want to see his brats. He told her to leave, and then walked away.

She returned to the motel with the children and felt like her gut had been torn into pieces by his rejection. She had hoped that the separation would help their marriage.

It was at that time, when she gave up all hope. Her hurt had turned into hate. She realized that no matter what she did or did not do, this marriage had no future.

Her primary focus was on her children's well being; she knew that she would have to make many personal sacrifices for her children's sake.

Ben had been working two part time jobs thirty-five miles apart on the Pacific Coast Highway. She found a small two-bedroom home that would accept four children.

Ben's cousin brought their furniture to them in his large semi-truck. Because it was such a light load, their few possessions were damaged when they arrived.

Barbara looked for a job that she could do and still be there for her children. She got a job cleaning vacant rental properties. She was able to work at her own pace and keep the children with her when they were not in school.

The company that she was working for had several homes for sale that were reasonably priced and in good areas. She learned that they qualified for a California veteran loan at a low interest rate.

Ben wanted her to apply for low-income housing. This would have put them in one of the worst areas in the city.

They finally agreed to buy a four-bedroom home in a good area near an elementary school.

Barbara's employer asked if she had ever considered going into real estate. She was in need of help liquidating her partnerships and corporations.

Barbara had reservations about passing a real estate exam with her limited education.

She was surprised when Ben approved and encouraged her to go for it, providing that she did not neglect her duties at home. She signed up at a prep school and used all of her spare time studying for the state exam.

She arranged for the children to stay with an aunt shortly before her exam date.

The night before the test, she got a call that Joel had an accident and was in the hospital. She was reassured that it was not life threatening and was encouraged to go ahead with the test the next day.

She took the exam in Los Angeles and drove 250 miles to the hospital. She was certain that she had failed the test.

Soon after she arrived at the hospital, she learned that Joel had a fractured pelvis in five places. When she was finally able to bring him home, it took months for him to recover.

The antibiotics that Joel was taking for his kidney problem stopped working. She found an urologist from UCLA who gave him a 50/50 chance of successful surgery.

She prayed night and day, begging and bargaining with God to take care of Joel.

She could not believe it when she got a post card from the Real Estate Commissioner saying that she had passed. She sent for her license and prepared for work. She was one of the youngest licensed agents in Southern California.

When she started real estate, they did not have sales training available so she had to learn through trial and error. With all the company inventory of homes, she was an instant success. The market was good and the properties sold themselves. All she had to do was to show up and draft the purchase contracts. She loved sales and the money that she made.

She was in the right place at the right time.

Barbara's self-esteem and confidence grew through her real estate activities. For the first time in her life, she had a sense of worth. The more money she made, the harder she worked. She took advantage of her professional friends and emulated them. She maintained a facade about who she was, what she had, and whom she knew.

She loved everything about the business. She enjoyed previewing homes and seeing how families communicate and lived.

She thrived on acceptance and the validation that she received from the public relations representatives and her clients. The respect and love that she got from her associates and community helped motivate her. Being young and attractive was to also to her advantage. Her success depended on her being assertive and knowledgeable.

Work became a game; the more she gave the more she got back. She would have months when everything she touched turned to gold.

When the market was slow, she looked for property to buy. She loved the challenges in real estate, win or lose. If sales were down, she would regroup and push harder. She had huge expectations and high financial goals. She took pride in achieving and loved the highs and lows in sales. She went out of her way to offer excellent service to her clients. She viewed herself as a hard-working professional, who was one of the top producers in her area.

She signed up at the Jr. College for continued education classes that the state real estate commissioner required. She took advantage of the many seminars. She believed that the more she learned, the more she could earn.

While working for a developer, they did own loan packaging and processing. She learned about creative financing.

She had a passion for real estate and loved every demand. She had vision and believed that she was investing in the future. It also became her escape.

After many years of marriage, she was able to purchase some extra items for her home and herself.

Ben complained about every penny that she spent on herself and improvements she made to the home. He protested when she got new drapes, or had bookcases installed and a new front door. She bought herself a nice diamond wedding band to replace the $7.00 band that Ben had bought her when they got married.

When she bought a used record player, he made a big fuss because she would want to buy records.

There was no music or laughter in their home.

When she came home from work, she would find Ben on the couch in his under wear watching TV. The children were ignored and running wild. The house would be torn apart and in turmoil. The children were without guidance or discipline.

She was expected to have dinner on the table at 6:00pm. If she came home late from work, she would catch hell. She had to schedule her appointments around Ben's demands. She knew that she could not depend on him to lift a finger to help her.

Ben refused to turn off the TV when it was time to eat. The children would grab food and fight throughout the dinner. When she was done serving the family and able to sit down to eat, everyone disappeared. She would clean up the kitchen and if she was lucky, she could get a few minutes to relax before she had to start on other chores.

Quite often, she would go to bed after mid-night. They slept in a double bed that was shared most of the time with one of the children. She was forced to sleep on the edge with very little room to move around. On many occasions, she would sleep in one of the kid's empty beds or on the couch.

She would cry herself to sleep with frustration and fatigue.

She was constantly told what a rotten mother she was. Ben would criticize, condemn, complain and blame. She does not remember a kind word coming from his mouth about or to her.

She would put on her real estate hat and go into the city where she was respected and needed. The more her career accelerated the more jealous Ben got. He refused to take an interest in the investments and lay on the couch, admiring himself with a mirror.

Ben was a time bomb, constantly ready to explode. The harder he yelled, the harder she worked and the longer she would stay away from home. He would sulk for months and at times, all she heard from him was a grunt.

Her goal was to buy one house a year. She managed to acquire quite a few investment properties. She did all the painting, cleaning and making the rentals ready after they became vacant.

She had some medical problems and her doctor prescribed Valium. When she got home at night, she would pop a couple Valium to help her cope. In the morning, she would take a diet pills to get her day going.

She spoke to an attorney about a divorce and had a good idea what it may involve. She was concerned about the affect that a divorce would have on her children.

She did not know how much longer she could take the abuse. There were times that the hatred was so strong she felt homicidal and suicidal.

Ben said that he was never going to change. When it became obvious that he was beginning to lose control over her, he tried to turn the children against her. He told her that he did not care what she did, that he would never let her have his kids.

Ben opposed all the values that she was trying to instill in her children. He encouraged hostility and defiance. He took pleasure in teasing and turning the kids against each other. Two of the children were Ben's favorites and he rejected the other two.

He was a bad influence and a negative example as a parent. Barbara resigned to the attitude of indifference and a house divided. It was just a matter of time before she would call it quits.

*****

She changed offices after the inventory was sold and worked for one of the top company's in the city. They were aggressive and active with the Board of Realtors. As their star producer, she continued to love the attention and activities.

She was limited with the amount of time that she could spend with her new friends. On occasion, she would meet her real estate friends at a dinner house after work for a drink. They would share lies about all their big deals. She had to be careful not to smell of booze or stay out past dark.

Barbara asked some of her real estate friends over for a get together. She wanted to show her appreciation for all that they had done for her. Ben rebelled by inviting some people from his work. His friends were vulgar, rude and insulting. Her guests made a quick exit, leaving her feeling humiliated.

With the help of a client, Barbara got Ben his first real job with a major corporation. Their new department specialized in similar work that Ben had done in Michigan. She gave her client Ben's letter of recommendation that he passed onto management. When they called, Ben got upset at her. He did not want to go in for an interview. After protesting, he agreed to go to the interview. He was hired shortly after.

She questioned the money that he was making and believed that he was holding back. His paychecks were always very small.

They had very little social life together. A nasty couple who were Ben's friends would come over on weekends to play cards. She was expected to play to win, regardless of how brain tired she was. She would be yelled at if she did not play her cards right.

It was hard for her to sit there and listen to conversation filled with obscenities. She struggled with what integrity she had.

*****

Barbara discovered a suitcase full of pornography and found some items in Joel's room. She got sick when she saw this. It explained what Ben was sharing with his friends in their bedroom when they came to visit. It also explained why he had such a sick concept about sex.

She knew that she could not take much more silence, mental, emotional or sexual abuse. She was black and blue from being hate f**ked.

She was constantly being accused of being unfaithful and called names if she looks at another man. She increased the Valium and her thoughts of suicide and homicide increased. She was emotionally dead inside.

*****

She was treated like a slut at home and a lady in her career. She lived a double life.

She was trapped between two worlds. She went to the ocean and decided to take a swim as far out as she could, wanting not to return. She felt the water sucking her under when she was caught in a rip tide. She let go and began to feel relief from everything. Somewhere and somehow a hand reached out for her, She fought back, not wanting to be saved. Again, the hand came after her and brought her out of the surf, coughing and disappointed.

She never knew who the person was that brought her out of the ocean.

*****

Ben got upset because she was making more money than he was. She took delight in seeing him getting pissed off about something that he could not control.

One evening, while playing cards; Ben kicked her from under the table for making a bad move. She jumped up, threw the cards across the room, and announced that she wanted to go home.

When they got home, Ben went to bed without saying a word. She sat at the edge of the bed while he pretended to be asleep. She got the courage to say, that she wanted a divorce. To her surprise, Ben jumped out of the bed excited. He said that he had been expecting this and reassured her that he would cooperate.

The next day she saw an attorney, who started the divorce proceedings. They agreed on the property settlement and child support. She did not want to kick Ben out right away. She feared that he would explode or change his mind. She agreed to his staying until one of the rentals became vacant or he found a place.

Two weeks later when he realized that she was serious, he moved out into an apartment close by.

The children were fourteen, thirteen, eleven and nine.

Ben's only concern was who was going to take care of him when he got old. He insisted on coming around at night looking for his vagina. When he touched her, she felt nothing but disgust. She was no longer his slave and would never let him abuse her ever again. His night visits stopped.

Ben was confident that she would come crawling back to him. She was determined to make it, or die trying. Barbara had been married for fifteen years.

The abused child was the abused wife.

CHAPTER 3

Looking for Love

Barbara was happy about being on her own for the first time in her life. She did not have any plans for the future other than taking care of her children and working. It was important for her to make it on her own, no matter what. She got $300.00 a month in child support and knew that she would have to make up the difference in order to support her children.

She was working at an office that was family owned. The owner's son, Mike, was the manager and administrator. She confided to him about her pending divorce. She wanted him to be aware of her situation. She was given reassurance that she had his support and help.

She knew that she had to stay motivated and focused. Mike became a friend and took a personal interest in her work. They would preview homes together and had an occasional lunch to discuss real estate. They had a very compatible and comfortable working relationship.

Mike was gentle and soft-spoken. He looked much younger than his thirty-seven years. He had never been married and was living at home with his parents.

When it was certain that her marriage was over, Mike asked her to go riding with him on his motorcycle. She agreed and went for a ride into the mountains.

She could not remember the last time that she had been able to spend a day having fun. She invited Mike to dinner to meet her children. It was important for her to be able to trust him around them.

Mike's visits became more frequent and the children seemed to like him. She started to look forward to his visits. There were times that she could not see enough of him. Her heart began softening and she thought that she might be falling in love with him.

She was starved for love and affection.

The property that she had worked so hard for was divided in half with Ben. She learned that Ben had more interest in the properties than what she thought. He knew exactly what they had and what properties he wanted. She did not fight him and thought that this was a small price to pay for freedom.

Her loneliness and sadness began to fade away. She was happy when she was with Mike. She did not question him and went into the relationship with blinders on. Her heart took control of her head.

She was told that if she could find a man who would accept four children, she had better grab him. She began to think seriously about what kind of stepfather he would make. There was a time when she thought that Mike might be gay. Sex was not a major part of their relationship and he did not make any advances toward her in that area.

She wanted to share the rest of her life with this man.

Before the divorce was final, Mike asked her to marry him. She accepted and they started making wedding plans.

She wanted her wedding to be one that she could remember the rest of her life. Their first conflict was where and how they should get married. He was Catholic and the church did not approve of his marrying a divorced woman.

She would have to prove that her ex-husband was a pagan and never baptized. The Church charged her $275.00 to annul her marriage with Ben. Six months after she re-married, they received the annulment and approval from Rome.

On March 3, 1973, they had a large formal wedding at the Lutheran church.

Barbara's three girls were junior bridesmaids and her son walked her down the aisle. Barbara had beautiful custom-made dresses. There were about 250 of Mike's family and friends at the wedding. Barbara had very few friends or family that she could invite.

After the wedding, her new mother-in-law had a beautiful garden reception.

They had not made any special plans for a honeymoon. They took off in her Cadillac after the reception without any special destination. They drove to San Diego where they got a motel room. Once settled, she realized how hungry and exhausted that she was.

They went to a restaurant near the motel. It was over dinner when she learned that Mike was expecting her to pay for the honeymoon too. She was disappointed but determined not to spoil the moment. After learning that Mike had never been out of California, they went to Las Vegas.

Mike moved into her home with his clothes and toys. His mother was anxious to have him leave and immediately put up a room for rent sign.

Their major conflict was over money. Neither of them had discussed in advance, who would pay for what. When she started asking questions, Mike told her not to worry. The first thing that he wanted her to do was to open a joint checking account. She agreed and gave him complete control over their finances.

About a month after they got married, Mike told her about a new housing development on the hill in the next city. She had not thought about relocating her family. She went with him to check out the new homes.

She liked what she saw and thought that it would be a good move for their new life. The area and schools would be much better for her children.

Using the money that she had gotten from the sale of her home, she put down a deposit for the new house. They took title together giving each of them a half interest and the rights of survivorship.

When she tried to discuss finances with Mike, he continued to be evasive.

She later learned that Mike was seriously in debt and could not help her with the necessary improvements for the new house. She was disappointed and concerned about their financial arrangement.

Mike told her that he was going to have an attorney draft an agreement that would make her a partner in the family real estate business.

Mike had his eye on another new house in the neighborhood that he also wanted to buy. She agreed to the purchase of a second house. She liked that house better because it was a single story.

She was forced into selling her two small rental homes near the beach. Unless she wanted to fight City Hall, she had to let them go for redevelopment. She wanted to buy two replacement homes with the money that she received from the city.

While she was studying for her real estate broker's license, she asked Mike to watch the market for good deals on properties.

Mike found two small, older homes that were for sale. When it came time for her to sign the final papers, she noticed that they were in both of their names. She did not want to start a fight with the man that she loved, so she chose to let the deals go through.

After the Catholic Church gave their approval, they remarried in the church. Her heart was not into it and she began to have serious doubts about their marriage.

She learned that in the first year, Mike made $2,600. This was used to pay on his debts. The issue of money was ignored and she began to question Mike's honesty. She realized that when she commingled her assets, it gave Mike permission to take advantage of her.

Mike was a man of a few words. He did very little around the home or work.

She began to notice that he was lacking motivation and ambition. In many ways, he was a boy who loved to play and added to his toy collection.

She paid for all the fun that they had skiing, riding dirt bikes and traveling.

It became obvious that she had become his mother and business partner. Mike could be very defiant and obstinate. He was a procrastinator and avoided taking responsibility; this was very frustrating to her.

Mike got close to her children who loved him. He was very immature and could relate at their level. He thought it was funny when one of the children would get into trouble.

*****

She passed her state exam for her real estate broker's license. She was proud of herself for completing the classes that the state required. Having her broker's license could open doors for her.

Mike was very intelligent and a graduate from UCLA. He studied the material that she had provided for his real estate broker's license. He passed a few months later.

They decided to have a big party with friends, associates and neighbors. They hired a live band and provided plenty of food and drinks. About seventy-five people showed up.

Someone in the neighborhood called the police complaining about the loud music. An officer came to the door and asked them to turn the music down. The police were concerned that her teenagers were having a party. She reassured the police that she would take care of the situation.

About fifteen minutes after the police left, the band started up again and did not tone it down as she had asked. The police returned a second time with three squad cars and a patty wagon. Their front yard was lined up with police officers telling them to shut down. This time the police did not leave until everyone had gone home.

They were having a blast and the guests were not happy about having to leave early. A couple of their friends got in the police officers' faces, protesting. It was touch-and-go as people staggered away from their party.

After the event, she did not give any thought to the situation. One of the guests was so offended that she wrote a letter to the editor of the local newspaper accusing the police of harassment. The chief of the police responded to her letter.

That was not how she intended to announce their achievements to the county. Later several people commented that it must have been one hell of a party and they wished that they had been invited.

It brings a smile to her face when she thinks about that crazy night.

*****

Barbara's schedule was very demanding when she went back to work. Mike and the kids would run away from responsibility. Her cries for help were ignored. The children played their father against their mother. This was to their advantage so they could do whatever they wanted. Neither one of them knew what was going on with the teenagers most of the time. The Kids did not understand what "no" meant. She was pressured into giving in to their demands.

When she tried to find out what was going on when they were at their dads, she was told that it was none of her business. The lack of communication left the door open for the teenagers to run wild. They were at the beach partying and staying out all night with friends. It was very upsetting when she saw her beautiful babies missing school and being destructive. She was frustrated, knowing that she could not do anything about it.

*****

Mike was being very secretive with his comings and goings. She got a call from a bank telling her that she had won the Boy Scout raffle. She gave her ticket stub to Mike so that he could claim the prize money for her. When she asked him about what she had won, he said nothing; she knew that he was lying.

She got a call from Mike asking her if she would like to adopt a newborn baby. After thinking about it for a few days, she agreed to adoption, if it was meant to be. Mike's cousin who was childless was outraged. They wanted a baby and had been trying to adopt for years.

She did not think anything would come of this and seriously doubted that the mother would just walk out of the hospital alone. All contacts with the mother went through Mike.

She was surprised when the hospital called to tell her that they had a baby girl waiting for them to pick up. She was not prepared for a baby and had to rush out to buy baby stuff.

The baby was beautiful, she She held back emotionally knowing that in the first six months the mother could take her back.

She stayed home and took care of the baby for a couple months.

Mike was being distant and not communicating with her. She wanted to be involved or informed about their finances. She was clueless with what and where she stood in that area. Mike kept the bank statements at the office. When she asked about money, he kept telling her not to worry, that they were okay.

She insisted on a full accounting of their joint income and expenses for the last three years. She refused to endorse her checks over to Mike until she got some answers.

Three years had passed and Mike had not kept his promise to give her an interest in the business. He acted as if he was hiding something from her. He spent a lot of his time on the phone when he was home in the evening. When she asked who he was talking to, he said that it was business.

She began to be very concerned about their relationship and tried to find solutions. She loved the man and did not want the marriage to fail.

She suggested that they take a belated honeymoon vacation to Hawaii. She made reservations for a week at the Club Med resort in Kauai.

*****

The Sunday morning, on the way to the airport, a Harley Davison chopper that was going over ninety miles an hour hit them from behind. Her Cadillac surged forward and the trunk popped open. She could see the man hanging onto his bike for dear life.

They had plenty of time before their scheduled flight was going to leaving for Hawaii. They waited for the police and ambulance to arrive. Once the police report was taken, they were free to leave. Shaken, they tied the trunk down and drove to the airport.

She called her insurance company and told them about the

accident. They reassured her that they would take care of it and wished for them to have a good time. She could not stop feeling concerned for the biker and called the hospital where he had been taken. To her amazement, his injuries consisted of a fractured back and a broken eardrum. When the biker heard that he had run into a Cadillac, he found it amusing.

*****

They settled in at the Hanalei Plantation where the movie *South Pacific* was filmed.

It became obvious that Mike was mentally absent. He acted as if he was home sick. He bought a couple post cards and filled them out. She asked him who he was sending them too. He pulled away from her. They slept in separate beds and he rejected her affection. He would wander off by himself and could not wait to get back home.

She began to panic over the coldness in their marriage. She contacted the Lutheran pastor who married them about marriage counseling. Mike agreed to go with her for counseling. She expressed her frustration and need for help in resolving their differences.

Mike spoke to the pastor first. After she had spent time with him, he told her, "to get rid of him." She was devastated and did not understand what had gone so terribly wrong. Her heart was breaking; she loved this man so very much.

Mike would go on over night trips in the motor home. When she asked him where he had been, he said that he was with "an understanding friend." She wanted to be his friend and could not understand why he could not talk to her. She gave him space, believing that it must be hard for him to adjust to a baby, four stepchildren and a wife.

She had become friendly with a neighbor who lived behind

her. Like herself, she was alone a lot waiting for her husband to come home. They did a lot of drinking together and got drunk just about every night. Drinking seemed to help relieve her frustrations.

Before this, she would have a beer or two and seldom ever got drunk.

She continued to pressure Mike about finances. Her personal savings and hard-earned money was almost gone. Each day she got more upset with Mike's avoiding the issues and his lack of accountability.

She was feeling very old, tired and used up. She was thirty-seven years old.

On a Saturday in October, when the baby was eighteen months old, the front door bell rang. When she opened the door, there were two very attractive women asking for Mike. She invited them in and called him to the door. He introduced her to his "understanding friends." It had never crossed her mind that he was seeing another woman.

He took the women around the house, acting like a real estate broker. He made comments about the decorating and other features in home.

Barbara approached Mike and asked him what was going on. He ignored her and continued talking to his friends. She wanted the women to leave; he told her that this was his house too and he could have his friends visit. The woman turned to her and said, "Why don't you f**k off?" and Mike laughed.

Her heart exploded and she knew that the marriage was over. She had been morally betrayed; the emotional pain caused her insides to explode. Her heart was breaking and she felt like, she was dying.

She had given all of herself to this man. She had been financially raped.

*****

As she prepared her escape, Mike wanted to take her car in to be serviced. She thought that this was a rather unusual. She agreed to let him take her car.

She knew that she could not take the baby with her; she decided to give Mike custody.

She rented a house in Santa Maria about 100 miles north from where she had lived.

On her trips back and forth over the mountains, she had problems with the power steering and breaks on her car. She had trouble controlling the car and bringing it to a stop. She took the car to two different mechanics for repairs. She continued to have the same problems. The third time, she took the car to a new mechanic who found a small hose that had been cut. After that had been fixed, she did not have any more car problems.

She realized that when Mike took an interest in her car, he was sabotaging her. The children's lives could have easily been lost in an accident.

She remembered the time when she got very sick and Mike took her to the hospital. She thought that she was having an appendicitis attack.

They were not able to find anything wrong with her. She thought that it must have been food poisoning. Mike could not get away fast enough after he left her at the hospital. She wonders now, if he had done something that made her sick.

Another time when they were riding on Mike's motorcycle, she almost passed out from the bike fumes. When she complained and almost passed out. Mike stopped and adjusted a hose.

BARBARA JEAN

Mike moved his girlfriend and her children into her home a few days after Barbara moved out...

CHAPTER 4

The Insanity

Barbara was emotionally and mentally devastated.

She could not work in the same office with Mike, even if she wanted to. The career that she loved and worked so hard for was gone. She signed up with a local real estate office in Santa Maria but could not get her heart into it. Her drinking was getting in the way of her work and her work was getting in the way of her drinking.

It tore her apart when her family scattered. Joel was a senior in high School and stay with friends. She took the three girls with her, who were upset about moving.

Another half of her investments was signed over to Mike. She had planned to use the money from the properties for her children's education or for retirement.

They had the same attorney who was indifferent toward her. God only knows what crap Mike had told him. He tried to get her to pay alimony and child support.

She stopped making plans for tomorrow. Absolutely nothing mattered anymore. She had serious doubts about her future. She did not want or care if she lived or died. Death would have been a relief from the emotional pain that she was suffering.

She had been a social drinker who could have a drink or two. In the past few months, she started to drink more and had to drink to relieve the pain that she was experiencing.

She drank so she did not have to feel what she was feeling.

She started going to the bars to escape the loneliness. She was a social drinker who had become anti-social.

She went from daily drinking to where she had to drink. She would take a drink and then the drink would take her. She was so in control that she was out of control.

It was at this time that she crossed over the invisible line into alcoholism. Drinking was her solution. Every dream that she had ever had was shattered. Poor me, pour me another drink. She needed every drink that she ever took.

She was consumed with hatred. She hated everything and everyone. She knew that she was in trouble. She had always been able to get back on her feet and put it together. She could not see any hope or options. She was dead inside. Her heart was like a rock.

It became obvious that her girls were having a hard time. She was in the bars every night and the children were left at home alone. She had made a down payment on a new home in their new city. Her teenage girls were unhappy about being away from their friends. They hated the Christian school that they were attending.

She canceled the purchase of the new home and decided to move back into one of her rental properties. She completely refurbished the home so they could be comfortable. Becky and Jan went to live with their father. Susan stayed with her.

She believed that this was probably for her children's best. Her mental and emotional condition was at a new low. She was thinking seriously about taking her life. She was not very optimistic about her future. She kept the hole in her gut filled with whiskey. She was thirty-six years old; she would eat, drink and be merry and hope to die.

She read in the newspaper about a singles group. She got juiced up so she could check it out. The last thing she was looking for was a man. She kept her distance from the singles and watched them having fun. All she could do was cry.

Almost every night they had an activity. She met other singles who enjoyed socializing and drinking. She looked forward to the parties. She could get drunk and nobody noticed. She would be the first to show up and the last to leave.

She never knew how the night would end or with who she would end up with. She would usually get drunk, slide down the wall onto the floor and pass out. Many nights she would sit in the corner sucking on the bottle, crying.

One night a well-dressed older gentleman came to a singles get together. He seemed withdrawn and reserved as he checked everyone out. She spoke to him about an after party at a local bar. He agreed to join them and sat next to her. He offered to buy her a drink. When she ordered her favorite drink, he ordered the same. He was her kind of man; they made very compatible drinking partners.

She learned that the man lived a couple blocks from her house. He told her that his wife had died three years ago from lupus. He shared how lonely he was. She felt sorry for him and understood his loneliness. He needed to be needed and she needed someone to take care of her. She welcomed his kindness, attention and offers of help.

He wanted to be more than just friends. She was not able to make a commitment to him. She wanted to be free to drink and party. He was a good man and she believed that she was not deserving of such a man.

She wanted him to understand that she was not able to make any commitments because of her past. She was surprised when he asked her to marry him so soon after they had met. He promised her the world and told her that she would be his queen. He insisted that their life together would be wonderful and reassured her that he would take care of all her concerns. She was losing control and needed him to take care of her, so she accepted.

They had a nice, private wedding with his boss as the best man. They spent a few days honeymooning in Mexico. He was a pleasant man and comfortable to be around.

They had a dilemma with two homes; she did not want to let go of her home. Neither one of them wanted to give in, they could not agree about which house to live in. He still had his wife's clothes in the closet. The bedroom door was kept closed and the room was the same as when she left it. .

She tried but could not find room for a ghost and herself. He had a major problem with her children; he did not approve of them being so disrespectful. After a couple months of marriage, they decided to have the marriage annulled. There were too many issues between them that were causing conflict.

They agreed to continue to see each other and to be friends. Dick was a good example of what a man should be. He had class and polished her rough edges. She was not capable of loving anyone or anything.

They did a lot of serious drinking together. She played sick emotional games with this man. It was damned if you do and damned if you do not. Their drinking usually ended up with them fighting about nothing.

She was a real nasty bitch to this man. She would have had so much to give if she had met him five years earlier. She needed him to be her anchor.

They remarried for the second time in Tahoe. She sold her home and he cleaned out the closet. They completely remodeled and redecorated his house. They had a fabulous view of the Pacific Ocean from every room.

There was a wine cellar built into the hill and a well

stocked bar in the family room. When she went to the market for a new supply of booze, she would tell the checker that it was for a party. They had many parties with just the two of them.

They suffered in comfort.

They did a lot of traveling while living the high life. They had twin motorcycles that they drove on weekends. He had a new Porsche and she had a new Cadillac. Money was not a concern.

She kept her distance from her children. She did not want them to see what a slobbering drunk that she was. She was afraid of what she might say or do around them.

Dick wanted her to have a baby for him. This would be impossible because she had her tubes cut and tied. He could not accept other people's children because he was so desperate to have a child of his own.

She began to notice that Dick was loosing it when he drank. He could not remember what happened the night before. She became very concerned because she needed him to take care of her, not her to take care of him. She began to think that he was an alcoholic.

A friend mentioned that she needed to go to Al-anon or AA to have her questions answered.

She wanted to know what an alcoholic was. She called AA for information. The woman who answered insisted on her going to an AA meeting with her. She did not have a clue what AA was or was not.

She knew a man from the singles group "One Again" who did not drink; he told her that he was in AA. Many years before, one of the PR, people talked about some of the bad things that he had done when he was drinking. He told her that he was in AA and did not drink.

The woman she called picked her up in an old ugly car and

took her to an AA meeting. They went up some dark stairs to a room that was filled with smoke and people. She could not hear much of what they were saying. She could not believe what she saw!

She was anxious to get home and have a drink. A nice girl like her did not belong in a place like that. The woman loaned her a stained blue book. She told her that the answer to all of her questions could be found in there. She offered to pick her up the next day for a meeting.

She felt sorry for the pathetic people that she saw. She was definitely not one of them.

The woman called a couple times trying to get her to go to a meeting. One day she called and asked if she could pick up her book. She could not imagine what made this book so special.

When the woman arrived at her door, she got the book. She asked if she had read the book, and she told her, "no." The woman got upset with her and told her that she was an alcoholic and going to die in her pretty house. She responded by telling her where she could shove it.

She concluded that Dick was an alcoholic and that there was no future for them. He was broken and could not be fixed. She had to get him out of her life, so she filed for a divorce. They sold their beautiful home and each bought condominiums within a mile of each other. They continued to run back and fourth sharing toddies and bodies.

She could not deal with life, others or herself. It was obvious that she was not going to be able to get it together this time. Drinking no longer did it for her.

She hid out and started to make plans to self-destruct. She put herself into many dangerous situations hoping that someone would snuff her out. She would sit in the chair for hours beating on her body making it black and blue. The physical pain helped stop the mental and the emotional pain that she was suffering.

She continued to be consumed with hatred and remorse. She had her phones turned off and would not answer the front door.

One evening while she was listening to her hurting and hating music, she had a moment of clarity. She remembered the words from the AA woman, saying, that she was an alcoholic and was going to die in her pretty house!

She knew that she was dying inside and that the party was over. *She would drink and could not get drunk.*

She lived in a different city and hoped that AA would be better there. She picked up the phone and called an AA number that was in the newspaper. The answering service transferred her to a woman who was taking calls for AA. The woman asked her if she had any alcohol in the house, which she did. With that response, the woman gave her telephone number and told her to call back when she was serious about getting help. She thought, what a bitch, but kept her phone number on her kitchen counter.

Several days later, out of desperation, she made another call for help. The woman asked her again if she had any alcohol in the house, which she did. She told her to take the bottle, get on her knees and pour the alcohol down the toilet and say, "God help me."

She did what the woman told her to do. She went to the bathroom and got down on her knees. She poured the bottle of whiskey down the toilet and said, "God help me." She was 41 years old and at that desperate jumping off place.

*****

THE BOTTLE by Linda Adams

I pulled the bottle out of the bag; it is almost gone
Desperation and anger flood my soul, I wanted to make it last longer
I see the reflection of my aging face and try to cover it with make-up
I see an empty shell of who I really am; my bloodshot eyes show my pain
I pull the bottle out and pour it into my glass; I put the poison to my lips
I will feel better soon and I do! Numbness floods my whole being
I can handle things better now; the emptiness is filled for a little while
The morning hangover makes me see the naked truth of it all
I feel so alone and wonder how my life has come to this
I long to get help but fear grips my heart
If I can no longer numb it all, I may go crazy
I pulled another bottle off the shelf in the store that knows me well
Embarrassment and anger strike me as I pay for it again
I drive back home in silence, the sound of it deadly
Fear of reality grips my heart as I realize
That I am an alcoholic

CHAPTER 5

A New Beginning

March 7th, 1981 was the first day of Barbara's new life without alcohol, "one-day at a time."

She arranged to meet the woman who had responded to her call for help. It seemed like time had stopped while she waited for help to arrive. They went to an AA meeting on a Sunday evening at 7:30.

✳✳✳✳✳

When Barbara came into the rooms of AA,
She wondered what the strange people were about.
They' were not drinking and they appeared to be happy,
She thought that she wanted out!
She was scared and did not know why; she was scared out there
She felt the walls surrounding her and that nobody cared
She couldn't drink and she could not stop, is this beginning or the end?
All she knew was that there was a time when the bottle was her friend
Her stomach cramped and her head hurt from nights of sorrow
Is she there for yesterday or is it tomorrow?
An earthquake dwells inside her and she thought that she was insane
She wanted to drink; she needed to drink to take away the pain
That is just how it started, one is not enough
She was there at least; "God help her" it is going to be rough
One day at a time, keep coming back, that is what she heard them say
It worked for them, it should work for her, and this has to be the way
Author Unknown

✳✳✳✳✳

She entered a smoke filled room with a long table. She was very uncomfortable seeing so many people mingling. She was introduced to a couple of people and directed to a seat at the table. She wanted to be invisible. She was not interested in being sociable.

The woman who brought her to the meeting was evasive and avoided her questions. Instead, she told her about a blue book that they called the "Big Book" and told her that the answer to all of her questions was in the first 164 pages of the book.

She remembers the time when the woman lent her a blue book. She thought that the book must contain some secrets to staying sober!

She felt like every eye in the room was checking her out. Her gut was cramping with anxiety and her head felt like it was going to explode. She was over-whelmed with fear. Mentally and physically, she was a basket case.

She was introduced as a newcomer. They insisted that she raise her hand to identify herself as being new so that they could get to know her. When she raised her arm, it felt very heavy. She scoped out the room, hoping not to see anyone who knew her. She was so full of fear, shame, remorse, guilt, anger, and hatred. She felt like there was a huge hole in her gut. The people in the room were very different from the people that she was use to being around.

She could not see how AA meetings were going to help her to stay sober.

She was surprised when they opened the meeting with the "Serenity Prayer." The people around the table introduced themselves and read some rules. They talked about their drinking and tattled on themselves. She could not believe what she was hearing. She knew that she would never tell anyone things like that about herself, especially with a group of strangers. As she listened to their sharing, she began to feel paranoid. They were putting into words what she had been thinking and feeling. She hated herself and did not want anyone to know about her past.

She listened to their horror stories and began to think that she was not that bad, she was different from them.

When her ears opened, she heard the words of hope and gratitude, something that she knew very little about.

Someone asked her if she wanted to talk. She was shocked when the words, "I am an alcoholic" coming out of her mouth. Her eyes filled with tears and her throat closed with emotions. Yes, she is an alcoholic, even if she did not have a clue what that really meant.

It surprised her when the room clapped after her admission.

When she got back to her empty house, she processed what she had seen and heard at the meeting. She knew that she could easily go to the liquor store and buy more scotch or vodka if she wanted; or she could return to the AA club in hopes of finding someone who could give her some answers.

She chose to return to the club where she met a kind woman who listened to her for hours and tried to answer her questions. She was encouraged to buy the Big Book. When she returned home, she was unable to comprehend or read the book.

She was at a crossroads to either stick it out with AA or die, she had a choice and debated her options and concluded that she would not drink and would give AA one-year. For her, alcohol would be a death sentence.

No matter what, she could not take the first drink. She was not to drink a drop regardless of what was going on in her life. She had to trust the strangers, as if her life depended on it. She was told that if she did not stay with AA, they would refund her misery.

*****

IF WE KEEP DRINKING

We will know a new imprisonment and new misery
We will relive the past and will not be able to shut the door on it
We will comprehend the word conflict and we will know pain
No matter, how far down the scale we have gone, we will sink even lower
The feeling of uselessness and self-pity will deepen
We will gain interest in selfish things and lose interest in our fellows
Self-esteem will slip away
Our whole attitude and outlook upon life will suck
Fear of people and economic insecurity will multiply
We will intuitively know how to run from situations, which never used to bother us
We will suddenly realize that God would have never done to us what we are doing to ourselves.
Are these extravagant promises? We think not!
They are being fulfilled among those of us who are still drinking, sometimes quickly, sometimes slowly.
They will always materialize if we keep on drinking.
Author Unknown

*****

She was a physical mess with her liver swollen and bloated from the fluids that her body was retaining. She had severe stomach cramping, sweating and shaking. She could not sleep or think straight. She was filled with anxiety and fear.

She de-toxed at the tables of AA and went to meetings and more meetings. It was hard for her to sit for a full hour without having to get up and move around. The people were so under-standing and patient. They would just say, keep coming back and don't drink.

There was no place for her to hide or run to and she did not trust herself to be alone. The Club and meetings replaced the barn and the pool hall where she once hid in. The first 90 days she was in a fog most of the time.

*****

WHY BARBARA DRANK

She drank for happiness and became unhappy
She drank for joy and became miserable
She drank to be outgoing and became self- centered
She drank for sociability and became argumentative
She drank for friendship and made enemies
She drank to soften sorrow and wallowed in self-pity
She drank for strength and became weak
She drank medicinally and got sick
She drank for relaxation and got the shakes
She drank for confidence and became uncertain
She drank for courage and became afraid
She drank for assurance and became doubtful
She drank to stimulate thought and blacked out
She drank for conversation and could not remember what she said
She drank to feel heavenly and came to know hell
She drank for power and became powerless
She drank to erase problems and saw them multiply
Author Unknown

*****

She kept her distance from the people in the fellowship. She did not want to get close to anyone. She was afraid that if they really knew her they would reject her. She was not in the program but around the program. She thought that the fellowship and the meetings was the program.

She was told to look for the winners; she did not understand what constituted a winner. She thought that a winner was anyone who did not drink.

It was explained to her that if she wanted recovery she would have to take certain steps. If she just stopped drinking, she would be a dry drunk. Nothing would change and she would continue to be miserable with no defense against alcohol and could drink again. .

When she referred to "her program", it was brought to her attention that she did not have a program. She later learned that the program was spelled out in the Big Book and the 12-steps. There was so much that she did not understand. There was no logic to their way of thinking.

On a couple of occasions, she went out for coffee after meetings with some AA members. She was very uncomfortable with their negativity. She began to understand what she did not want and went on a search for winners.

She began running into people that she knew from real estate and in the singles group. One old friend told her that he was saving a seat for her. He asked her, "What took you so long?" She saw another man that she knew and expressed her surprise at seeing that he was one of them. He remarked that he did not know for a long time that he was one of them.

Word must have gotten out that she was in recovery. Never once did anyone judge or say anything ugly to her. They wanted to offer her their unconditional experience, strength and hope.

She became suspicious of their motives and concluded that they were her guardian angels. Her phone began to ring at home with sincere, concerned friends. One friend took her to meetings and spent many nights sleeping on her couch while she was detoxing.

They encouraged her to eat sweets and ice cream, the sugar helped with her cravings. She was also encouraged to take vitamins, especially super "B." She drank and ate a lot of citrus. She was advised to stay away from virgin drinks that taste similar to what she had drank. She was told to change where and how she had did things so that her old patterns could be broken.

After thirty days of not drinking, she was given a token. It was a little pewter key chain with thirty days stamped on it. It was the longest and hardest thirty days of her life.

Her skin broke out something awful from the toxins that were in her body. Most of swelling went down and her eyes began to clear up. She continued having anxiety attacks and problems sleeping.

She started to feel a little more comfortable with the meetings and people. There were days when she would hear something that she identified with. She would leave the meeting upset and angry over what she had heard. She believed that they were looking in her window or reading her mail. There were many days when she wanted to quit but could not because she did not have anywhere to go.

The more that was revealed, the more restless she became. It was suggested that she get a sponsor/mentor. She could not trust anyone and doubted if she could get honest with another person, especially a woman. She had very few woman friends. She loved men in spite of all her life's experiences. She talked to one woman about being her sponsor and all she said was, "Don't drink and go to meetings." She must have realized how very sick she was and did not want to rock her boat.

Barbara managed to stay employed for a company that did repairs for off shore oil companies. The good old boys were just that. They were drunk most of the time and did not notice that she was no longer one of them. When she told them that she had quit drinking, they began to give her a rough time.

One day after work, she discovered that someone had puked on her new car. She gave notice and found work with another offshore company in their accounting department. She had a nice, private office that she could hide out in and focus on staying sober and going to meetings. She was an anonymous employee.

To this day, she does not know how she was able to do her jobs before or after she got sober.

Around ninety days sober she began looking and feeling good. Her life involved work and meetings. She began thinking about some of her old-drinking friends.

She had heard about a party and decided to check it out. She invited a man from AA to go with her and bought a six-pack of Pepsi. In her old grandiose way, she parked her car on grass in the front yard. It was not long after that the house was filled with people. They did not seem very happy about seeing her there. Her stomach started to cramp and she knew that it was time for her to leave. Her car was blocked in; she could not get out of there fast enough.

She was torn and confused about her before-and-after-life. A part of her wanted to play and the other part told her that the party was over. She had to change her playmates and playpens. She needed to think the drink through and remember what the drink had done to her.

She had to concede to her inter most self that she was a real alcoholic. She could talk the talk but she could not walk the walk. She had to make a gut-level decision if she wanted to be sober more than she wanted to be drunk.

She took an AA friend to a bar that had a great band and dance floor. When they opened the door, the smells of booze and cigarettes came reeking toward them. She told her friend to pretend that we were drunk and nobody would know the difference. After one dance, they had to leave. God was giving her a very strong message and she conceded that her life was unmanageable.

She realized that alcoholism is a disease that destroys people mentally, emotionally, physically and spiritually. Alcoholism is an allergy similar to what she has with shellfish. In spite of how much she loves shellfish, she knows that she had to stay away from it or become deathly ill.

She began to experience and understand what the second part of the first step really meant. She realized how her emotions could be cunning, baffling and powerful. Her two experiences were examples of how easy it is to lie, deny and justify. It would be suicide for her to continue messing with the miracle. She had to remember that she had a disease that wanted to kill her.

*****

ALCOHOL

I am more powerful than the combined armies of the world.

I have destroyed more men/women than all the wars of the nation.

I have caused millions of accidents and wrecked more homes than all floods, tornadoes and hurricanes put together.

I am the world's slickest thief. I steal billions of dollars each year.

I find my victims among the rich and poor alike, the young and the old, the strong and the weak.

I loom up to such proportions that I cast a shadow over every field of labor.

I am relentless, insidious, and unpredictable

I am in the home or the streets, in the factory, in the offices, on the sea and in the air.

I bring sickness, poverty and death.

I am your worse enemy.

So if I do not care about you and bring so much misery and pain, t hen why do you still care about me?

Author Unknown

*****

She was encouraged to sign up with the Navy's alcohol abuse program. She agreed and discovered how very little she knew. Her intellect was not going to keep her sober. If she could not understand something, she would reject the information. When she kept hearing the same message repeatedly in AA, it became harder to ignore.

The meetings opened old wounds and had an emotional effect on her. She started to feel things that she did not want to feel. The committee in her head would take over when she processed the information. She would obsess repeatedly about the what, when, where and why's. Her head kept flashing back into the past. She was told to accept the things that she could not understand. She was a victim!

There was a woman who had been sober a long time who she later asked to be her sponsor. She told her that she would be her friend but could not commit to being her sponsor. As hard as it was for her to reach out and trust, she opened up to her. She barfed out the garbage that she had been carrying. The woman kindly listened and told her that she did not know what to do with her.

Several months prior to getting sober, Barbara had booked a trip to Mexico's Yucatan with a travel group. Against the advice of her AA friends, she decided to go. She had a few months without a drink and was confident that she could control herself for a week. She justified her trip with her interest in archeology and wanting to see the Maya ruins.

She slept one night at the Atlanta airport on her way to a hotel in Cancun. Once she was settled in her room, she froze up with fear. She became emotionally crippled and angry with herself because she could not drink. She could not wait to get back home. Once back, she confessed to her friends that they were right, she should not have gone. She became more teachable.

When she checked her messages on her answering machine, she had several calls. One call was from an old friend, Lynn, who was hysterical and begging for her for help. When she returned her calls, she learned that Lynn had committed suicide. She immediately began beating herself up for not having been home to answer her calls. She became depressed thinking that she could have made a difference...if only.

Her AA friends were not very comforting. They would say, "For the Grace of God there go I."

She would be driving down the road and out of nowhere; she would go into a rage over something that had happened in her past. She would have to pull over to the side of the road and say "The Serenity Prayer." She would take several deep breaths before she continued with her day. Her prayers were desperate and intense. She had a hard time accepting people, places and things.

The expectations and demands that she put on herself were very unrealistic. She did not trust herself and was living from heartbeat to heartbeat. She was so full of grief and remorse. Poor me, reality really sucked...She was in an emotional war with herself.

She began to understand what the second step. She did not think that it applied to her until it was explained that insanity is doing the same thing over again but expecting different results. Insanity would be picking up the drink. Insanity was her inability to live in reality. Everything that she was learning was in conflict with what she had believed.

Drinking was no longer her problem, now her problem was her thinking.

She began to feel like she was getting sicker and started to withdraw from AA. She realized how twisted her thinking was and didn't like reality. She had so much to unlearn.

The friends who had carried her the first few months began cutting her loose. She had become too dependent on them. She was forced to make new friends.

She became depressed and filled with doom and gloom. The AA pink cloud and honeymoon was over. She did not know who she was and when she began to get in touch with herself, she did not know what to do.

She had to face reality for the first time in her life. She started to think that AA was not going to work for her. She was told that she needed to find a Higher Power that God could and would if sought. The God of her understanding would get her drunk.

Her life and soul depended upon her finding a Higher Power. She went to the cemetery daily for a couple weeks where her friend Lynn was buried. She watched the people standing near a new grave; she thought that they must have really loved that person. The next day she saw a young girl alone at the same gravesite. On another day, a hearse brought in someone and the cemetery caretakers lowered the body into the ground. When she was watching the activity at the cemetery, she was thinking about her own demise.

She was desperately trying to connect with God in prayer. She knew that drinking was no longer an option. She was miserable and depressed

She was sick and tired of being sick and tired. She was convinced that she was doomed and began planning to end her life. She gave up on God.

She laid back in her car seat with the sun shining on her face. Out of nowhere, she heard a voice saying, *"let the dead bury the dead, get on with living I am with you."* She felt a warm flow of energy come through her body. She was given the peace that passes all understanding! She had a profound spiritual experience.

✼✼✼✼✼

She realized that she was God's Kid

She left the cemetery feeling that everything was going to be okay. She realized that there is a God or Higher Power. There was no doubt that she was given God's grace and validation. She was able to feel a warm spiritual touch and healing of her spirit.

She did not understand God, but it no longer mattered. She came to believe that there is a power greater than her who would restore her to reality.

The faith that she had was so small and her God was so far away. This was the beginning of God's Kids spiritual search. Her faith was very fragile; she had to let Him do His thing and give up control.

She had many unresolved issues with religion. At times of conflict, she felt like a hypocrite. She was not comfortable with religion. She had faith in whatever it is or is not. The miracle in her life and with others was positive proof that it just is...

*****

DON'T BE FOOLED BY ME

She wears a mask, a mask that she is afraid to take off
Pretending is an art that is second nature to her
She gives you the impression that she is secure
That all is sunny within as well as without
That confidence is her name and cool is her game
That she is in command and that she needs no one
Beneath lies no smugness, no compliance
Beneath dwells the real her in confusion, in fear, in aloneness
She panics at the thought of her weakness and fears being exposed
That is why she frantically created a mask to hide behind

BARBARA JEAN

A facade to help her pretend, to shield her from the glances
However, such a glance is precisely her salvation, her only salvation
This is the only thing that can liberate her from her own self-built prison
It is the only thing that will assure her
That she is really worth something
But she doesn't tell you this, She doesn't dare, She is afraid to
She is afraid that your glance will not be followed by acceptance
Your laugh would kill her
She is afraid that deep down she is no good and that you will reject her
She plays her game, her desperate pretending game with a facade
The parade of masks and life becomes a front
She idly chatters to you in the suave tones of surface talk
She tells you everything that is really nothing
You have to hold out your hand even when that is the last thing she seems
     to want
Only you can wipe away from her eyes the blank stare
Only you can call her into aliveness
Each time you are kind, gentle, and encouraging,
Each time you try to understand because you really care
Her heart grows wings, very small wings, very feeble wings but wings
With your sensitivity and sympathy and your power of understanding
You can breathe life into her; she wants you to know that
She wants you to know how important you are to her
How you can be a creator of the person that is she
You alone can break down the wall behind which she trembles
You alone can remove her mask
You alone can release her from her world of panic and uncertainty from
     her lonely prison
Please do not pass her by
It will not be easy; a long conviction of worthlessness builds strong walls
The nearer you approach her, the blinder she may strike back
It is irrational but despite what the books say about women,

She is irrational
She fights against the very thing that she cries for
However, she has been told that love is stronger than strong walls
And in this lies her hope, her only hope
Please do not beat down the walls with firm hands but with gentle hands,
For a child is very sensitive
Author unknown

*****

Without a sponsor, she decided to self-sponsor. She wrote what she thought was a fearless and moral inventory, and decided to share with a Lutheran minister. She made an appointment with him and provided him with information about the fifth step.

They met and she spent several hours spilling out her guts to him. It was hard for her to talk about her secrets that she was going to take to her grave. She continued until she was empty and there was nothing more to say. She had to take several breaks because of the tears and crying.

This was the hardest thing that she had ever done. After she finished, the minister asked her, "Now what do we do?" She told him that she would like to go to the church alter and pray with him. After she left the church, she felt like her insides were bleeding.

She tried to focus on doing the next right thing but could not let go of all the crap that she had shared. She became even more depressed.

She contacted her doctor and asked for sleeping pills that were not a narcotic. He told her that there was no such thing. She had him call in a prescription. After she picked up the prescription, she put the pill bottle on her kitchen counter. A friend asked her about the pills. She told him that they were sleeping pills. He took the bottle and flushed it down the toilet. She was told that no one had died from the lack of sleep.

She was paralyzed by depression. She wanted to hide under the pillow and suck her thumb. She got a call from a friend asking her if she was going to the AA Convention. She did not want to go anywhere or do anything.

Shortly after the call, her doorbell rang. When she answered it, the friend told her to get ready; she was going to go to the Convention. Under protest, she got dressed and drove to the Civic Center. After being in a crowd of over 1,000 AA members, she had to escape.

On her way home, she stopped in front of a liquor store and sat in her car. She could hear the voices of AA saying, think the drink through, do not ever forget how awful it was, do not take the first drink, we will refund your misery.

She drove out of the parking lot without going inside to buy a bottle. When she got home, she got down on her knees and prayed.

The hardest thing for her to learn was to ask for help, she did not have a problem helping others. When she focused on other people's problems, she could forget about her own. The lack of trust and pride kept her from reaching out. She loved seeing or being a part of other people's miracles.

She was becoming very sensitive and her feelings would go from mad, sad, glad, hurt, and afraid to lonely within fifteen minutes. Intellectually she wanted to be able to understand everything; her intellect continued to be her enemy. It was impossible for her to trust God completely when she could not trust others or herself.

She was a rock and an island for most of her life. For many years, she could not laugh or cry. The first time she really laughed, it startled her.

Everything in her life was a big deal. When she was told that, there were no big deals, it upset her. She had not been able to stay focused in the moment. She was always out there somewhere, either in the past or in the future. She began to understand when she took it "'one day at a time," it helped her to stay focused and in reality. This not only helped her with her drinking but with her thinking.

She heard someone say that if she had one foot in tomorrow and another foot in yesterday, she was peeing on today. When she stayed in the moment, hour or day it was easier it to face what was in front of her. She discovered that it was impossible for her to get goofy when she took it one day at a time.

Many of the AA slogans were very helpful to her attitude adjustment. Especially, easy does it (but do it)...When she took it easy she was not as compulsive or over whelmed.

Learning to have an attitude of gratitude was also hard for her. If she had made a list of what she was grateful for, it would have been very short. Filled with remorse, it was impossible for her to be grateful. It made her sick when she heard people say how grateful they were.

She remembered an older man who once told her that he loved her. Afterwards he asked, "I bet it has been a long time since anyone has told you that you are loved?" She could not remember the last time when she was told that she was loved.

She heard the people in AA; say that they would love her until she could love herself. She did not know or understand what love was.

She continued to spend all of her spare time in meetings. She was fortunate to live in an area of California where there were meetings at one place or another day and night. She would sort through what she heard in the meetings. There were many times when she would bolt out of the room, vowing never to return. Knowing there was no other place for her to go for help, she would return.

They talked the disease to death. She was told to listen to learn and to learn to listen. This was not easy for her to do.

There were certain people who shared in the meetings that she would tune out.

She learned to listen to the similarities and not the differences. She had to ignore the messenger and focus on the message. Acceptance did not come too easily for her. She was told to read a page in the Big Book on acceptance twice a day for 30 days. When she completed the assignment, she tore the page out of her book.

She got vitamin B shots to help calm her nervous system. She continued to battle depression. The cloud of doom and gloom did not go away in spite of what she did. She could not let go of the grief and remorse...

She tried to sell the program and avoided talking about herself. She was told, that we do not sell sobriety we live it. That was a big blow to her ego. She was a parrot and could repeat what she had heard. After that, she, clamed up and seldom spoke at meetings. She was compromising her sobriety with pretty words. She had learned to talk the talk.

It was a huge relief to learn that she was not in AA to get good but to get well. She had many years of destruction and abuse that was not going to go away over night. She had to learn to save her ass and not her face. She was only physically and intellectually sober.

God has a lot of over-time work to do with God's Kid. She was told that she was to well. She had put up a front most of her life and did not know how to act sober. Pretending definitely had been second nature to her. She had built some very strong walls over the years. She was afraid of being venerable and hurt. She does not suffer well.

She was beginning to resent some of the people in AA. There were days when she had to sit out of eye contact of certain people. When resentments festered it was a strong indicator that there is something inside of her that she needed to look at.

She had unrealistic expectations of her God. She needed to be rewarded for being good and not drinking. She wanted God to do for her what she could not do for herself, that included just about everything. She thought God was getting old and tired from helping all of His kids. She quit praying.

*****

She got up early one morning and rushed right into her day
She had so much to accomplish and she did not have time to pray
Problems just tumbled about her and came heavier with each task
"Why doesn't God help me?" She wondered, HE answered, "You didn't ask."
She wanted to see joy and beauty, but the day toiled on gray and bleak
She wondered why God did not show her. He said, "But you didn't seek."
She tried to come into God's presence; she used all of her keys at the lock
God gently and lovingly said, "My child you didn't knock."
She woke up early this morning and paused before starting her day.
She had so much to accomplish, that she had to take time to pray
Author Unknown

*****

She tried to understand what she did not understand. She would defend herself on principles when she did not have an idea what they really were. She had taken what she learned out of context. She took over God's job by trying to play God.

She agreed to turn her life over to a Higher Power but continued to hang onto her self-will. She admitted that she was powerless in some areas. It was clear that when she drank, she could not predict the outcome. She had walked down a destructive path; wanting someone to do for her, what she could not do for herself. She wanted out of her misery. It is a miracle that she was still breathing!

She wanted the pain to stop. She found a new source of pain when she got honest and saw reality. She was resentful toward everyone and everything that had ever touched her life. She could not forget and forgive. She could no longer blame others for her experiences. She had to take full responsibility for everything that she ever did or didn't do.

She got angry with AA for tricking her. All she wanted was to stop drinking and did not realize that she was going to have to change her entire life.

She was sick and tired of being sick and tired. Enough is enough she cried. She was dying inside and unable to walk the walk. She prayed to be willing to be willing.

God's Kid started to look for a man to fix her and help relieve her loneliness.

She met a man who had all the qualities that she admired. He was good looking, well dressed, intelligent, drove a Cadillac, had a job and was in sales. She gave him permission to take over her life and the keys to her house.

She discovered that the man was very controlling and secretive. He would go into violent rages, breaking things and yelling. She became afraid of him and withdrew.

She realized that she was in serious trouble with this man and had to get him out of her life fast. She suspected that he was on heroin, bi-sexual and had a prison background. She questioned his identity and believed that he was not who he said he was.

She told him that if he did not leave, she would call the police. When she mentioned the police, he panicked and could not get out fast enough.

She later learned that her suspicions were true and that he had a history of being violent toward women.

By the grace of God, she did not drink, one day at a time, for a year. God truly looks after fools and ex-drunks! She did her very best, considering what she had to work with. When the day came for her to celebrate with the Group, she was in a lot of emotional pain. She made it to the podium and accepted the medallion with her four children sitting in the audience. When she spoke, she said, "That she was told that there were no big deals and that everyday had been a big deal."

Her grandson, Keith, was born shortly before she got sober. She was able to watch him grow. She identified with the little guy; they were both babies learning to walk.

She was once told to observe the elementary kids at a school playground to see if she could relate. When she did this, she could identify.

Her four children were supportive of her recovery. There were times that they did not like her being in meetings so much. They wanted to collect from her, the time and attention that they were deprived of for so many years. As a family, they were very dysfunctional in many ways.

Joel and Janice were married and they both had children. Susan was on her own doing well and Becky was a teenage mother living with her father.

God's Kid had many expectations for her children's lives. They did not turn out as she had planned; she was not what they wanted her to be either. Her children did not understand that she was fighting for her life, her sanity and recovery.

She had to take care of herself; this seemed selfish. She was without any coping skills and was having a hard time handling responsibility.

Her phone did not ring with loving hellos from her children. They felt even more rejected when she had to say "no" to them. Her buttons were broken and she could not live with guilt and manipulation.

Her children had never seen her treated with respect; therefore, they did not know how to show respect. She did not like being around her children because of their attitudes. It was going to take a long time for them to forgive and forget her for what she did not do...

Sadly, her new friends treated her with more kindness then her own children. She had to give them the right to be wrong!

She prayed for the day when the family would heal and their relationship would be filled with love and respect. She had to give them the freedom to be themselves.

She prayed daily for strength to keep walking, talking and believing. It becomes obvious how sick she was when new revelations were reveled. She was aware of how quickly the insanity could return.

There were times when she was emotionally trapped and had thoughts of suicide. She kept suicide as an option if all else failed. She no longer had drinking as her option. She had to pray to God daily for his help in removing her suicidal thoughts.

She was not a very patient woman and wanted it all NOW. She learned that the power of identification and example had a strong influence on her. She could see miracles in others lives but not her own. She had to exercise her spiritual muscle! When she had God in her life, she had balance. She wanted her God back.

*****

One evening she saw an older man who appeared to be very frail. When she looked into his eyes, she could see fear. She asked him if he was all right. He told her that he had just gotten out of the hospital. Without thinking, she asked if he is terminally ill. He told her that he has black lung disease. She asked, if there was anything that she could do to help? He told her that he wanted to talk with a man in AA. She bought one of the Big Books and gave it to him. She asked him to return the next night and promised to find someone for him at the Club.

Unfortunately, she was unable to find anyone to help him. They met and she took him under her wings. He wanted to know about God. She gave him all the strength and hope that she had. She answered his many questions and prayed with him.

A week later, he was back in the hospital's intensive care unit. She visited him briefly and saw the book that she had given to him on the table next to his bed. She brought in a minister with her who was in AA. The man surrendered and put his life in the hands of God.

She attended his funeral a few days later. She asked God, what' is this all about. It was so unlike her to race against time to help a dying stranger.

A friend asked her if there was someone or a situation in her life that reminds her of the man. Her father came to mind; she did not give him comfort or love when he was dying from lung cancer...

The stranger, made it possible for her to do what she could not have done for her father. She realized that her response could be a form of amends.

CHAPTER 6

Risking Change

God's Kid has a friend who was in the Navy and return-ing home from Spain. He was anxious to see her and wanted to make plans for their future together. He asked her to pick him up at the airport and join him at this ranch in Utah.

She reluctantly agreed to go with him. She was laid off from work and had a lot of free time.

She told him about the commitment that she had made to AA. He had seen her drunk many times and did not hesitate to tell her to, "Go for it." There were times that he was her protec-tor and he had seen her good, bad and ugly side.

She had become addicted to meetings and found it scary when she left with someone who did not understand recovery. She arranged for a woman to stay at her house and to take care of her dog.

After she picked her friend up, they drove her car to Utah. When they got past Las Vegas, he asked, "How long has it been since you had seen your family in Michigan?"

He suggested that they continue to South Dakota where his mother lived after stopping at his ranch. He encouraged her to leave him in South Dakota and for her to continue onto Michi-gan. She remembered how unpleasant her mother was the last time that they were together; she did not leave under very good circumstances.

God's Kid thought that it was time for her to make amends

with her mother. After saying a quick prayer for courage, she called her mother. When her mother answered the phone, she said that she did not know anybody by that name. Then she asked, "What do you want?" She managed to say that she wanted to see her and to come home for a visit. This was a very profound statement coming from her. She did not think of the tiny village as home. She had rejected her mother for many years and now her mother was rejecting her.

She dropped her friend off in South Dakota and took her time driving to Michigan. When she got closer, she called her mother to let her know where she was. She had to let go and let God, believing that the result of her visit was none of her business. When she arrived on Church Street, she was greeted with a defensive welcome and a hot bowl of soup.

The tension lifted as they talked and shared. It did not matter how she felt or if she was understood or acknowledged, this was not about her.

She made herself as comfortable as possible and slept in her old bedroom. She could see the scars from family wars and realized that in spite of it all, this was home.

She gave all of her time and attention to her mother's many wants and needs. She took her places; they laughed and became friends. Behind her mother's aged blue eyes, she could see the soul of woman who had paid her dues in life. She felt empathy toward her mothers many struggles and realized that she did her best, considering what she had to deal with, even if it sucked.

She knew that she had to accept this old woman with all of her personality flaws, rough edges and demands for endless attention. She had only one real mother and nothing could change that. She had no choice other than to accept her just as she was and to love her unconditionally.

She went to the old farm where she had once lived and walked the railroad tracks that she feared as a child.

They attended the old Baptist church together where she saw some of the same old women, who were sitting in the same seats, that they had sat in for the last fifty years. She looked around inside the church and admired the beautiful interior.

Her mother had been the church treasurer for many years. When she was younger, she would help her mother and help herself to the collections. Stealing from a church and being a thief bothered her. She knew that she had to pay the church back. When the collection plate came around, she returned the money that she had stolen.

She saw some of her old classmates who had rejected her and compared the differences in their lives. She no longer felt like white trash and did not have anything to prove to anyone anymore. They are okay and she was okay!

When it came time for her to return to California, she asked her eighty-five-year-old mother if she would like to return with her. She was surprised when her mother responded that she would love to go. She warned her that it would be a long five-day ride. Her mother said, "That there were many states that she would like to see." Her mother was excited and quickly made preparations before she changed her mind.

God's Kid was concerned about their relationship and the long days on the road together. Her mother was looking forward to seeing her grand and great grandchildren.

She took the trip one-mile at a time and stopped often for breaks. They went to bed early and got up early. She was prepared to deal with mother's stubbornness and was pleased to find her very flexible. They took a side trip to the Grand Canyon for a quick look. Exhausted and with the minimum amount of stress, they arrived safely in California.

When she arrived home, the house was a disaster. Her dog was almost dead from fleas and the lawn was dead. Someone had been sleeping in her bed and was wearing her clothes. All the food in her freezer was gone. Apparently, several people had been staying in her house while she was gone.

She was angry, with the woman who took advantage of her. She told the woman to leave. She had to pray away any resentment that she had against the woman, knowing that resentments could eat her alive. She could not do anything about what had happened. She was powerless!

Her mother enjoyed every minute of her visit with her grand-and great-grandchildren.

When it came time for her mother to return, she took her to the Los Angeles airport. She felt sad, thinking that this would be probably the last time that she would see her alive. She thanked God for giving her the courage to walk through pride and for doing what she could not have otherwise done by herself.

God's Kid had days when she was so lonely; she would cry herself to sleep. She was empty and ached for someone to hold her. She needed to find someone special who could care and share with her. She had been good and it was time for God to take care of her loneliness.

She believed that God wanted her to be happy, joyous and free.

She had been speaking before large AA groups and had most of the answers, she thought. She was becoming self-righteous and full of spiritual pride. She was in her terrible "two's."

She felt that God owed her; it was time for her to collect.

She spoke to a friend who told her that she was being very unrealistic with what she expected from a man. Her friend said that God probably had someone for her who is very different from what she thinks she wants.

She opened her eyes and what did she see, but "Eddie."

They had shared speaking engagements and did a lot of God-talking together. They had similar beliefs and commitments but very different backgrounds. He was Mexican/Italian, with a very small frame, illiterate and ten years old than she. He was a complete opposite of the kind of man that she would like. She invited him to move in with her, thinking that two can live cheaper than one. This could help them both financially.

God's Kid saw the man's potential and set out to fix him. His appearance was embarrassing, so she loaned him money to buy a new wardrobe. She got intimate with him to see if there was any passion. She felt guilty about sharing her bed with him and not being married. She was concerned about what her friends and family would think about their living together. She wanted to be a wife and believed in marriage.

They arranged to get married. He was unable to help financially. He told her that when he sold the motor home he would pay her back. She paid for the wedding, honeymoon and everything else.

After they got home, she did not feel very good about the marriage. She began to think that she had prostituted herself out of loneliness. She prayed to God for a miracle and asked for His help with the marriage.

Within the first month, Eddie quit his job. She would come home from work and he would be waiting for her to take care of him. He was a man of good intention but a procrastinator when it came to helping her. She became impatient after having to keep asking him for help.

He would pout and sulk, accusing her of putting expectations on him. Of course, she expected him to act like a caring husband.

One day when she came home from work, he introduced her to an insurance agent. He wanted her to take out a $50,000 life insurance policy on herself. The flags went up, especially when he told her that he wanted her to pay for the policy and he would be the beneficiary. After sixty-five days of marriage, it was clear that she had made a big mistake. She knew that Eddie had to go; it was time for her to bail out.

She rushed to the courthouse, got divorce papers, and filled them out. She told Eddie that it was not going to work out between them. She got his signature and packed him up. He moved back into his motor home. She went to a meeting and threw herself on a table, admitting that she had made a big mistake. She felt that God had let her down!

*****

God's Kid was at a meeting when she thought she had heard the voice of an angel. The woman was sharing her faith and hope without reservation. Her ears opened as her words fed her hungry soul. She listened to how and what the woman shared, receiving affirmation and comfort with what she heard. The woman's face glowed and her voice was gentle, soft and loving.

It was obvious that this was her messenger. She wanted what she had. She became very anxious to reach out to the woman and to ask for her guidance. She wanted to know her secrets. When the student is ready, the teacher will appear. She got the woman's name, Sharon and phone number. They arranged a meeting.

God's Kid was still trying to self-sponsor herself. She was three years sober. She was dying inside and needed this women help.

When they met, Sharon asked her if she would be willing to go to any lengths to stay sober. She asked if she would take directions and be rigorously honest. She would have to trust Sharon completely and give her control over her life. Was she ready? She replied with a "YES!"

*****

SECRETS

I keep my pain a secret; it is something that I hide
I do not want the world to know, so I lock them deep inside
Way down deep in a dark place it still grows
I think I can handle it as long as no one knows
My secrets have always been with me, I am not sure what that is about
I had to keep all the doors locked so the pain would not get out
I have been a warden for so long, I do not know who to blame
The way I keep my secrets safe is to wrap them up in shame
I add a few more layers to this secret that I cannot name
The secrets will not stay buried no matter what I have tried
The secrets I am hiding are not dead, I buried them alive
I do not seem to have the strength to fight the war
My secrets are escaping; they have broken down the door
They threaten to consume me in overwhelming pain
I fear that I may smother from all the shame
I do not think I am strong enough to face what has to come
I know that I need help, but what I really want is to run
I have been running all my life; my chances for escape are past
I must swallow my pride and admit that I am powerless, at last
Once I accept that on my own, I cannot deal with the pain
Only then can I be free from the secrets and have my life back again
I have found a place for others who hurt just like me
I must open my heart and allow love to set me free
When I share my pain, it keeps me from sinking too deep
I am as sick as the secrets that I keep
Author Unknown

*****

God's Kid was torn between religion and spirituality. She knew that she could not trust the God that she had known as a child. She did not want God to be a man because of her past relationships with men. She realized that she did not know anything about anything. She was still unlearning and having to set aside her old ideas.

She concluded that what she thought that she knew was probably a lie. Her God was still in the clouds taking notes and out to get her. She thought that God had given up on her or was lost.

She gave Sharon permission to be her Higher Power and allowed her to be her eyes. She found her God in and through her. Sharon had her write what she wanted her God to be. She wanted a God who was kind, loving, caring, forgiving, gentle and wise. Once her list was complete, Sharon had her read it aloud to her. She told that her to visualize God as being kind, loving, caring, forgiving, gentle and wise and nothing more or less. It was okay to create her own personal image of God and to forget what she had been taught.

When she prayed, she was to address her prayers to her loving, caring, gentle, forgiving and wise God and to ask for guidance and protection.

Sharon told her that she could not pray all her problems away. Faith without action is fantasy! God is very old and tired of listening to his kids babbling.

She helped her to put together a gratitude list. The only gratitude that she had was for her children. Sharon helped her to expand on a gratitude list. She did not realize that there was so much that she had taken for granted.

It became obvious that she had a lot to work ahead. Sharon had her look at her patterns, set-ups and pay-offs. How she had sabotaged herself with self-centeredness. She kept telling her that the ego has to be smashed, to the depth.

God's Kid went on a spiritual search. She began reading spiritual books. Sharon told her about "The Course in Miracles." She bought the books and could not believe what she was reading. The more she read the more she was able to understand about her inner power. She had it all backwards believing in an outer power. She was finally getting affirmation from the "Course."

Sharon made it clear to her, what God was not. She had to give up completely wanting to see, touch and feel and know what God is. She was doomed to repeating the past unless she changed. Men were her fix and as lethal as alcohol.

She remembered the day in the cemetery when she first met the spirit...of God. There was a presence and peace inside her. She had been rushing down the freeways of life, dodging Mack trucks. She was twenty-five miles ahead of God, yelling back for Him/Her to hurry up.

PEDAL

At first, she saw God as her observer, her judge, keeping track of the things she did wrong, to know whether she merited heaven or hell when she died.

God was out there like a President. She recognized his picture when she saw it, but did not really know him.

Later on when she recognized her God, it seemed as though life was rather like a bike ride, but it was a tandem bike, and she noticed that God was in the back helping her pedal. She did not know just when it was that God suggested that they change places, but life has not been the same since.

When she had control, she knew the way. It was rather boring but predictable. It was the shortest distance between two points.

When God took the lead, there were delightful long rides, up mountains, through rocky places and at breakneck speeds. It was all she could do to hang on, even through it looked like madness. God said, "Pedal!"

She worried and asked, "Where are you taking me?" God laughed and didn't answer. She started to trust, and she forgot her boring life and entered into the adventure. And when she would say, "I'm scared!" God would lean back and touch her hand.

God took her to people with gifts that she needed; gifts of healing, acceptance and joy. They gave her gifts to take on her journey, their journey, God and hers. And when they were off again, God said, "Give your gifts away, they're extra baggage, too much weight." She gave to the people that they met and she found that in giving, she received and still their burden was light.

She did not trust God to be, in control of her life at first. . .She thought God could wreck it, but God knows bike secrets. He knows how to make it bend, to take sharp corners, jump to clear high rocks and fly to shorten scary passages.

She is learning to shut up and pedal to the strangest places. She is beginning to enjoy the view and cool breezes in her face with her delightful constant companion, her God.

And when she is sure that she just cannot do anymore, God smiles and says, "Pedal."

Author Unknown

*****

God's Kid accepted a job working in accounting for the Ventura Townhouse that was a large retirement community. She started without any training and it did not take long before she realized that she was in over her head and had to learn fast. She was one of many who had been hired in the past few months. She was warned that the boss was very difficult.

The morale was low and the working conditions were very poor. There were many contradictions within management. After weeks of being put down and corrected over little things, she began to think about quitting.

One day, after being in the middle of her boss and the manager's disagreement, she announced that she was going home sick and that she was going to be sick for a long time. She had no intentions of returning.

She called Sharon and told her about how proud she was for having the courage to walk out. Sharon responded with an, "Ooh." A few days later Sharon called. She asked her if she thought she was going to let her get away with quitting. She had her write about her problems with authority and told her that it was God's job to close the door, not hers.

She was forced to look again at her pride and to see how she gave up without to resolve the situation. She had to inventory and get honest about her compulsiveness. She was instructed not to be a quitter and to stay until God closed the door. Her justification for leaving did not matter.

Finding a job had never been a problem for her. Sticking with it and admitting that she did not know it all, was a problem for her.

She found work with a major bank's new loan department. She was thrilled with the opportunity to work in finance. She made friends with the temporary manager and took advantage of everything that she could learn from her. They were a great team until a new manager was hired. When her friend did not get the management position and she was terminated, she was disappointed.

Her loyalties became twisted with the personalities and politics. She forgot who was signing her paycheck. She was called into the manager's office and given a termination check. She was devastated over being fired. This experience turned out to be another hard lesson that she needed to learn.

*****

God's Kid was returning home from an AA meeting when she saw Jim walking down the street. She recognized him from the meetings. She stopped and asked him if he would like a ride home. He accepted and as they were driving, he mentioned that he needed to find work and was willing to do anything. It was obvious that drinking and life had really beaten him up. She mentioned that she needed help with a couple odd jobs around her home. He seemed eager to help her.

Jim did some painting and maintenance for her. She offered to pay him, but he refused to take any money. He indicated that he was grateful to be able to help her. In return, she invited him to stay for dinner. This was the beginning of his many visits, hanging around to see what he could do for her. She had a comfortable friendship with the man. He had been in law enforcement most of his life. Drinking got in the way of his work and work got in the way of his drinking.

He was very handsome, gentle, spiritual and easy to communicate with and much younger than she. He began spending some nights with her and noticed that he was bringing in some of his clothes. She did not object and just let it happen. She knew that it she should not become involved with someone who was newly sober.

She loved making love with him. He made her feel beautiful and uninhibited. This relationship was a gift and she did not want it to end.

He attended Mass at the church everyday. He said, "That there were too many people in AA who knew him from when he was in law enforcement." He quit attending meetings. Instead, he attended mass at the Catholic Church everyday.

She offered him all of her band-aids and was willing to help him financially. She took the man hostage and believed that they would have a great future together.

She talked him into going to Las Vegas where they got married. He got his Private Investigator's license back and began working for local attorneys. He started to develop an attitude and wanted more independence while still being very dependent.

One day when she came home from work, she found him

on the couch drunk with beer bottles all over. He had been entertaining old friends and forgot that he could not drink; she was in shock with what she saw. She threw him out in his under-wear and called his friends to pick him up.

He returned a couple days later, promising to be good.

He was not able to stay sober in spite of how hard he tried to cover it up around her. He would romance suicide!

She got a call from Sharon asking her, "What's going on?" She said, "Nothing!" Sharon jumped on her for lying and told her not to BS her. She thought Sharon must have been looking into her windows. Busted, she had to tell her the truth about Jim.

Sharon told her that she knew what she had to do and asked her if she wanted to be sober or drunk. She replied, "Sober." Then Sharon asked her, "When are you going to take care of the situation?" She knew that it was either him or her; together the both of them could go down.

Sharon insisted that they meet in a couple days to discuss the problem. She was instructed to write about her relationship with Jim, especially where she was at when she first met him. Whenever she took an honest look at an issue, her stomach would cramp. She did not want to admit to the power that lust had over her.

She knew what she had to do, regardless of how she felt about the man.

If God intended for this man to be in her life, it did not matter what she did or did not do, it would be...

Once again, she went to the courthouse and got divorce papers. She filled them out and got them signed. She was very concerned about her liability with a drunken husband running around.

*****

She was angry at the disease after seeing how it destroyed so many good people's lives. The grief was over-whelming at times. She felt so powerless.

She hit a bottom with relationships.

God's Kid believes that God does really work through people. She had placed her trust in what Sharon said and her directions. Her self-will and old ideas were not working anymore.

There were many times when she did not want to take direction and got upset with Sharon. She was threatened, that if she did not do as she was asked, she could find a different sponsor. The thought of losing her help scared her.

She did not want to attend meetings at the Club. Instead, she preferred meetings where higher functioning professionals attended. She was reminded that the ego had to be smashed. She was no better; they were all God's kids.

She was instructed to attend meetings for thirty days at the mission where the street people went. She was told to listen to what they did not say and to open her heart. She protested until Sharon reminded her, that she had agreed to go to any lengths and to follow her direction.

She was very uncomfortable when she went to the new meetings. After attending for a couple weeks, she began feeling empathy and compassion for the people. Her heart softened and her eyes would tear up for the first time, when she felt what they were sharing.

She realized that she was one drink away from being on the streets but, "by the grace of God, there goes I."

Sharon had her write a list of what she wanted in an ideal relationship. She was told not to hold back on anything that she wrote. With deep forethought, she made a fabulous list of qualities that her heart desired. She assumed the reason for preparing her list was to present it to God like a shopping list.

She wanted him to be spiritually sober, emotionally and physically healthy, employed with benefits, own a truck or car, be financially secure, carrying no garbage, be loving, caring and kind, good looking and close to her age with a good body and Caucasian.

She was proud of her list. She met with Sharon and read to her what she had written. When she finished reading, she saw a big smile on Sharon's face. Sharon had her cross out "Mr. Right" and wrote her name at the top.

Sharon asked her if she could be what she desired in a man. She got upset for being tricked into "naming and claiming." She knew that it would be impossible for her to be everything that she desired.

She was told that she would attract what she was, "like attracts like." She did not know a thing about relationships. She was covered with emotional scars from walking across the freeways of life.

She used the list that she had made as a guide for living.

She was asked if she could stay single and out of serious relationships for five years. She needed to learn to be a friend to herself and to make friends with other women. She has always had at least one special man in her life since she was a teenager.

She made a major decision to change what freeways she would take.

When she was four years sober, she "TOOK" a third step with Sharon. She surrendered completely and gave God her will without reservation. She was convinced that her wants would destroy her. She needed to walk carefully with her eyes wide open.

*****

AFTER AWHILE

After awhile you learn the subtle difference between holding a hand and chaining a soul

You learn that love does not mean learning and company does not mean security

And you begin to learn that kisses are not contracts, and presents are not promises

And you begin to accept your defeats with your head up

And your eyes open with the grace of a woman and the grief of a child.

And you learn to build your roads on today because tomorrow's ground is too uncertain

And futures have a way of falling down in mid-flight

After awhile you learn that even sunshine burns if you get too much, so you plant your own garden and decorate your own soul instead of waiting for someone to bring you flowers

And you learn that you really can endure

And you learn that you really are strong

And you learn that you really have worth

And you learn and you learn. . .with every goodbye

Author unknown

*****

Her vacation was over. Financial desperation was setting in. She accepted an accounting job for a labor contractor who had over two thousand Mexican field workers on payroll. The office looked like a jail with bars on the windows. Everyone spoke Spanish except her. The owner would spend his nights sleeping in his office after being drunk. There were kids of the co-workers running around the filthy office.

The workers would hang out in the alley, drinking whiskey and shooting craps. She did not know what she would find when she went to work.

She called Sharon and told her about her situation. She told her to stay until God closed the door. What an order!

She was let go from her job. God must have said enough is enough! God is not very funny when it comes to teaching lessons.

This was the beginning of her new work ethics.

CHAPTER 7

Walking the Talk

God's Kid received a call from her brother Larry asking her if she could come to Michigan. Their mother was going into the hospital for surgery on a pinched nerve in her neck. Without the operation, she would not be able to walk. She was needed to take care of her mother after she is released from the hospital.

The timing was good with her being out of work again and available. She agreed to help and flew to Michigan.

When her mother got out of the hospital, she was in horrible pain. She was very upset and angry for having come through the surgery, mentally she was prepared to die. She had problems with balance and the doctors wanted her to move around and walk as soon as possible.

Her Mother refused to be helped and fought against her assistance. She slept on the couch so that she could be close to her mother in the event that she was needed. Her mother's excessive demands were very stressful. She was unable to get very much sleep. She felt like a frog jumping up and down to help her mother.

God's Kid reached her limit with the abuse and the unrealistic requests that her mother made. For the first time in her life, she blew up at her. She told her that she would have done everyone in the family a favor if she had died.

Her sister Wanda came up from Florida to relieve her. Thank God, she could not get back to California fast enough.

She was in financial trouble with the IRS, and owed an attorney, who had placed a lien against her home. She knew what kind of work that she did not want to do and began thinking about going into the counseling field. She loved helping others.

She volunteered to be on call with AA's hot line for women who were seeking help. She had called this same source when she needed help. Some of the women who called in, she would meet at an AA meeting.

She was still carrying around a lot of baggage. Her insides were not matching her outsides. She had learned all the pretty words. When she got honest with herself, she realized that she was sugar coating her sobriety.

Sharon told her that no matter what she had done she would still love her. This was a huge relief because she did not want to open old wounds. She had to let go of the past before she could move on.

She was told about the healing steps. She had doubts about her ability to be completely honest with herself before this. She was asked to write down all of her resentments of people, places and things, this include every aspect of her life.

The first resentment that she remembered was with her brother who buried her teddy bear under the apple tree. He kept telling her that he knew where it was. In the spring, he dug it up and gave it to her. She did not think about how this had affected her. Instead, she turned it into hatred toward her brother.

Sharon helped her to look at the causes and effects. The deeper she looked, the more she was able to understand. She could see how her security had been threatened. It was no longer about them. It was how she reacted and perceived things. She hated her brother because he took away the security and love that the bear represented.

With new insight, she was able to gain wisdom and face the enemy.

This did not make what happened to her all right. No one deserves to be abused and emotionally tortured.

God does not give us any more than we can handle. There were many times that she doubted that statement. She learned that God does not wear a watch and that his timing is divine perfection. He just knows.

Most importantly, she had to forgive all of her thoughts, words, deeds and actions. She could not forgive others if she could not forgive herself and accept that God had forgiven her.

Why was it so hard for her to forgive herself? If she should have, could have or would have, her life would have been so much better. Her grief and remorse was overwhelming at times.

When Sharon and God's Kid got together, they always said a prayer and invited God into their talks. This was not just one woman sharing with another. In their case, three was not a crowd.

Gods Kid wrote down a long list of resentment. One by one, they talked about them. The deeper that they shared, the more relief she felt. This was unlike what she shared with the minister. She felt detached; it seemed like they were talking about someone that they had once known.

God worked through this woman with her unconditional love, sincerity and gentleness.

The list that she made was for her healing, the responses were not important. She wrote several amend letters and cried when she was writing.

God's Kid asked herself how could she justify asking forgiveness for her thoughts, words, actions and deeds? They were the ones who owed her an apology; she was the victim.

She took her amends letters and walked a half-mile to a mailbox, crying all the way. She dropped the letters into the mail slot and returned home. She was surprised when she felt a relief.

She dropped to her knees and asked God to help her to let go.

The responses to her amends letters were varied. She was laughed at and told that she was being too hard on herself.

She thought that her actions would take care of all of her amends. Over the years she has

had several situations or people remind her that it will take a lifetime to complete her amends. When a person or situation developed that she needed to make amends to, she did not hesitate to make it right.

She will walk the walk being aware of her thoughts, words and actions.

God's Kid was ready to sell her home and risk changes in her life. Her house had been trashed and it was her skid row. She needed to make financial amends...

After the house was sold, she sorted, sold and gave away stuff that she had been hanging onto for years. While doing this, she saw the ghost of her past appearing before her. She was amazed with what she had been holding onto. There was very little that she wanted to keep. The physical inventory was a very emotional experience.

She had her children come by to take what they wanted. As they sorted through her stuff, they laughed and cried together.

She filled a box with toads that she had collected from her travels. She had hoped that one-day she would find a prince among the toads. One afternoon a boy about eight years old walked by and she stopped him. She asked him if he would like her box of toads. The little guy's eyes lit up. She saw one happy boy walking down the street.

What few possessions she had were put into storage. She made her financial amends and was free.

She heard about a counseling program in Wisconsin that

had an excellent training and internship program. She was very interested in learning more about what they had to offer.

She went to Michigan to stay with her mother until she could decide where and what she was going to do.

She submitted her application for counseling training and got a call for an interview. She drove to Wisconsin where she met with the staff. They gave her a tour of the facilities. She was told that they required a high school diploma.

She did not want to lie about being a high school drop out and asked if they could accept her if, she had a GED. They said yes. She told them that she did not have a GED, but would call them after she got it. She was forty-five years old.

She went to a Junior College in Lansing that did the GED testing and signed up. She found a bookstore that had a prep manual and began to study. She crammed and once a week she would take a test and pass.

On the last day of testing, the administrator asked her to wait. She thought that she must have failed. A man came into the room where she was waiting. He introduced himself as the college Dean. He wanted to congratulate her for passing and with such a high score. He seemed to be amazed with what she had achieved.

Once back in the Village, it hit her. How ironic it was for her to get a GED in Michigan after having been kicked out of school there. She had a smirk on her face, thinking that this was an amends to herself.

She could not help but think about the kids who have fallen through the cracks. She remembered her dad stressing the importance of getting a good education. He said that education is something that no one can take away from you.

She felt good and knew that she did not have to prove anything to anyone. She had finally gotten her own validation and approval. She had known for years that she was not stupid, but now she really knew it. God was smiling!

God's Kid's, mother was enjoying her visit and she was trying to be as loving as she could be. It was very hard to love the unlovable. She would attend church with her every Sunday and have brunch at a local restaurant with the beautiful old church ladies. She made a game out of spoiling her mother. She quit personalizing and internalizing when she was with her.

While at her mothers, someone came to the door who wanted to see her. She was surprised to see Dennis, her first love when she was sixteen. It had been thirty years since she had last seen him and he did not look much different, just older.

She flashed back to when he broke her heart. She was curious about how he had been over the years. He invited her to join him for dinner the next night. She accepted and agreed to meet him. It was hard for her to believe that he even knew that she was in town. His aunt who lives across the street from her mothers must have told him that she was there.

They met and he told her that he had just gotten out of a mental hospital after a breakdown. He was divorced after eighteen years of marriage and worked as an editor for a newspaper in Detroit. He asked her to follow him to his place. He was renting a little cottage at a lake. While there, they went for a ride on the lake in his rowboat.

Dennis remembered her as she was at seventeen and he seemed to be stuck in time when they were together. Neither of them could get past the past. She thought about getting even and playing him emotionally. Everything in her said...run.

She believed that there are no coincidences. Dennis was not on her amends list. This was a once in a-lifetime chance for her to forgive and let go. She told God that this meeting was not very funny! She was sure that God was laughing. She smiled.

Her brother Larry asked if she would like to visit their brother in Arlington, Virginia. It was in the fall and the trees were changing with beautiful colors. They decided to take her little Honda because of the great gas mileage. This was the first time that she had been with her brother alone as adults. She was excited.

She started talking to Larry and could not shut up. She had his attention and there was so much that she wanted to share with him. When they arrived at Leonard's she was talked out.

The mountains and hills were beautiful with color. It had been years sense she had seen trees that were so spectacular.

Returning home, they went to Kane, Pennsylvania where their father and his family are buried. They made sure that everyone was tucked in okay and paid their respects. Larry asked her if she was all right, she smiled and told him that she was okay.

They got a motel room in Kane for the night. She found AA and called them. She learned that there was a meeting that night next door to their motel. She asked Larry if he would like to go with her. She was happy when he said yes. At the meeting, she asked if it was all right for her brother to sit in.

They were welcomed by the twenty AA people who opened their hearts to them. They asked her if she would like to share with the group for a half-hour. They would share back the last half-hour. She was apprehensive about sharing with her brother in the room. She agreed and went to the podium at the front of the room. Once she got there, she did not think about Larry being in the room. She shared from her gut and gave very little thought about what she was saying; God took over...

The room shared back and her brother raised his hand. She had not told him that he could not participate. She saw tears in her brother's eyes when he raised his hand to speak. He said that he did not know that about her and told her that he loved her. He also said that he could see why she loved the AA people so much. She cried!

Her heart was so full of joy the remainder of their trip back.

The time had come for God's Kid to leave Michigan and go to Wisconsin for her counseling training. She had had such a wonderful visit with her family; she did not want to leave.

She had learned to love the little village of Fowlerville. The wonderful memories will be special to her for the rest of her life.

*****

She was enthusiastic about learning again after having been schooled out for years. She felt very good about her decision. She had high expectations and looked forward to the experiences ahead.

She arrived in Wisconsin in January after having spent her first holidays with family in many years.

Shortly after settling into what would be her new home, she was given another tour again of the facilities. The psychiatric hospital, treatment facilities, and resident houses were on five acres, off the banks of the Mississippi River.

She was assigned to a house that was on the grounds and occupied by female patients. She was asked if she would like to be the housemother and in return, she would be given a discount on her tuition.

She met six other trainees who had been chosen from over 250 applicants. She later learned that the other students were there on grants. Trying not to be judgmental, she was concerned about their qualifications. They acted more like patients than trainees...

The trainees avoided her and were very indifferent. She felt shutout and rejected.

Being from California was not to her advantage. Her strong belief in a Higher Power was not appreciated. She had been given the best room in the house while the other girls had to sleep in an attic. She came with a car that was full of her clothes. The other trainee's were poor and had very little. She came with money in her pocket and the love of her family.

It was a no win situation. The differences set her apart even though she did not feel she was any better than they were. Unfortunately, the trainee's did not see it that way.

Her first assignment was to sit in-groups with senior counselors and be an observer. She paid close attention to what and how the groups were conducted. She was getting anxious to get into the books and for classes to start so she could have some balance. When she inquired about the classes, the subject was avoided.

They were short staffed and more interested in having her work in the hospital for a minimum wage. This did not interest her as it did with the others.

The house that she was living in had been taken over by a wealthy older female patient. She had been their star resident on and off for years. It was obvious that this crazy woman was not going to give up control and let her be the housemother. The house was filthy and not fit for ten women to live in. She retreated to her room and ignored what was going on around her.

When she confronted the resident patient who lived in the house to help with cleaning, she flipped out on her.

When the weather permitted, she would leave the grounds. She had not been so cold in her life. It had been over fifteen years since she had been in a sub-zero winter.

After having been in Wisconsin for several weeks, they were signed up with the University of Wisconsin's continued education program. It did not take long to discover that they did not have qualified instructors or structured classes. When handed study material, the trainees acted as if it was a joke.

The training was constantly being interrupted to fill in with patient care. They were required to get up early to turn the grounds lights off and on at night.

God's Kid could see that this was a difficult situation. She started to feel depressed. She felt trapped, isolated and lonely. She became angry with herself when she realized what a mistake it was for her to be there. She began to feel tormented with confusion.

She saw that it was all about big business and not training. They were taking advantage of the insurance companies. They admitted people who did not need to be there. When they could not fill all the beds, they began recruiting troubled teenagers. There was a fine line between the staff and patient, depending on who was carrying the keys or what bed you are sleeping in.

She remembered what Sharon had told her about prostituting her sobriety. She was to give for free and for fun. She was not feeling free, nor was she having fun.

The counselors used Gestalt or B&D (brutalize and demoralize) with patients and each other. She could not be hard or tough on people; they had beaten themselves up enough...

She started to question her sanity. She saw things going on that were hard to comprehend. She had thought that she had seen it all until she went to the "Nut House."

She was beginning to think that she was going to loose it with depression, disgust and disappointment.

She began planning her escape. On April fools day she packed and stayed in her room. When she did not show up at the staff meeting, they came looking for her. The head co-coordinator came to her room. When he saw that she was packed, they had a meeting that she was told to attend before she left.

She joined the group and took a chair. She did not remember much of what was said. She had her made up her mind to leave in spite of them. After awhile she got up and prepared to leave the room. Before she walked out, she told them that she loved them and wishes them the very best.

After she returned to the house she had some of the patients load her car. She did not know where she was going or what she was going to do. She drove to Madison, Wisconsin and got a motel room. All of her disappointments, hurt and anger came out at that motel.

She decided to go back to Michigan to think things through. She traveled a couple of hundred miles in an emotional blackout. When she arrived in Michigan, she could not talk without crying. She got very angry with God.

*****

GOD SAID "NO"

She asked God to take away her pain, God said, "No"
It is not for me to take away, but for you to give it up.
She asked God to grant her patience, God said, "no"
Patience is a by- product of tribulations
It is not granted, it is earned.
She asked God to give her happiness, God said "no"
I give you blessings; happiness is up to you.
She asked God to spare her pain, God said "no"
Suffering draws you apart from worldly cares and brings you closer to me
She asked God to make her spirit grow, God said, "no"
You must grow on your own, but I will prune you to make you fruitful.
She asked God to help her love others, as much as He loves her.
God said. . .finally, you got it!
Author Unknown

*****

Does she stay or does she go back to California? Either way she would have to swallow her pride. She had a key to her mother's house and could stay there. Her mother was in Florida for the winter and was expected to return home in a couple weeks.

Her mom was not very happy about seeing her again so soon. She knew that she could not and did not want to settle in Michigan. It was time for her to move on.

A real estate friend of hers who lived in California who had won the lottery; wanted her to come to work for her. She bought a new Cadillac and returned to California.

She rented a small apartment and got most of her furniture out of storage.

She arranged to activate her real estate broker's license and went to work for her friend.

She was concerned about the reception that she would receive from her old business associates.

She was surprised with the warmest of welcomes. Her friends bent over backwards to help her to succeed and feel comfortable. She could see the love and caring in their faces.

She located a therapist who could help her with the rage.

She learned that it was not what she said or asked, that caused her pain. She was guilty by omission. She would pride herself on being honest, not realizing that through omission, she was setting herself up and lying. This would boomerang to either herself or others, causing a major communication breakdown. She had to learn that it did not matter so much what she said but how she said it. She had to overcome her pride and learn not be afraid of sounding ignorant. She was lacking the wisdom to know the difference. Blind faith was just that, blind faith! She would leap into the unknown expecting God to catch her.

Her mentor/sponsor told her to stand still and stop searching.

Once she got back at the desk, there was a lot of activity in the office with the press and the State Lottery. The media was promoting the winner and giving her a lot of attention. It was hard for God's Kid to do her job with so many distractions.

The winner's husband decided to run for City Counsel. He turned the office into his campaign head quarters.

She was caught in the middle and needed to make some money. She began thinking about opening her own office.

*****

She bought a nice Condo near the beach and leased office space. She prayed for freedom from financial insecurity. She used the last bit of her energy in this adventure. She enjoyed being back in touch with her real estate friends.

She became torn between helping herself and helping others; she had a hard time finding balance with family, friends AA and work

She had several women that she sponsored who had become very dependent upon her. Her work interfered with helping and helping interfered with her work. She had switched from booze to babies. She struggled financially and knew what she had to do if she wanted to be a success. It would require all of her time and commitment.

She was burning herself out at both ends, trying to be everything to everyone and leaving nothing for herself. She was once told that the most selfish thing that she could ever do, was not to give back what she had been freely given. She could not keep it if she did not pass it on. She felt guilt if she did not keep on giving, she was not in touch with her limitations...

The AA women were like little birds with broken wings falling at her feet. Their experiences were very different from hers, but yet very similar. She could see herself in their faces and remembered how hard it was for her when she did not have any-one to help her. She heard what they were not saying and never knew if she was going to be kicked or hugged by them. She could see their desperation and defiance.

She kept asking God to give her strength. She knew that if she did not help the women, they would most likely be doomed. Her motto was "save a life." She saw and heard things from the women that tore at her heart.

She would take them hostage and help them take the steps to recovery. There was a long road of reconstruction ahead for them. She felt an urgency to help them and share everything that she had. Together they walked in blind faith, realizing that they needed each other to survive. The more she shared, the more she would forget her problems. Like her, the women would get upset when they saw reality. They would leave upset, only to return a few days later with a little more surrender and willingness.

God's Kid believes that we never know when we are enter-taining angels. She has very fond thoughts of the women and feels privileged to have been their mentor.

She has seen tragedy and wept for the loss of some very dear friends, who forgot and gave up before the miracle. She was reminded of how powerful the disease is when she attended friend's funerals. She knows that this disease wants us all dead.

She continues to be amazed by the miracle that she has witnessed in some very special women's lives. To this day God has not let her down. He continues to guide, protect and direct her. They will forever remain very close to her heart.

*****

God's Kid was investing more into her business than what she was making. She was having female problems and rushed to the hospital. They gave her Valium and when she came to, she was loaded. The bitch was back!

She called an old friend and asked him to pick her up at the hospital. She wanted to get it on and party, instead they got something to eat. Her friend realized that she was in trouble and took her to an AA meeting.

While at the meeting, she proceeded to tell everyone off. The disease had progressed even when she was not drinking. Her old behaviors and attitudes reared their ugly heads. She was going to have to fight for her life again.

THE DISEASE WAS SAYING

I hate your meetings and your Higher Power. I hate everyone who has a program and who comes in contact with me. I wish you death and suffering..

Allow me to introduce myself; I am the disease of addiction. Cunning, baffling and powerful, that is me. I have killed millions.

I love catching you with the element of surprise. I love pretending that I am your friend and lover. I give you comfort and fill your loneliness. You called me when you wanted to die I was there.

I love making you hurt and cry. Better yet, I love it when I can make you so numb you cannot hurt or cry. When you cannot feel anything at all, gives me joy.

I give you instant gratification and all I ask is for your long-term suffering. You invite me in when things are going right in your life. You said that you did not deserve to be happy and I agreed with you.

People do not take me seriously. They take strokes, heart attacks and even diabetes seriously. They do not realize that without my help these things would not be possible.

I am such a hated disease and yet I do not come uninvited, you choose me. So many have chosen me over reality and peace. The more you hate me, the more I hate your twelve-step program that weakens me so I cannot function.

Now I must lie here quietly. You do not see me but I am growing bigger every day. I am here waiting until we meet again, if we meet again.

Author Unknown

Shortly after this experience, she had to return to the hospital for a complete hysterectomy. She made a point of telling them not to give her Valium or any drugs. She knew that she could bear the physical pain, but not the mental effects that the drugs had on her.

She was depending on her roommate, Grace, to help her when she was recovering from surgery. The roommate was in another world most of the time and of no help.

*****

God's Kid got a call from her brother, Larry, asking if she would take care of their mother in California, she was eighty-eight years old. She had been kicked out of a couple homes that took in the elderly; she was raising too much hell. Her mother was severely depressed and could not take care of herself. She was not eating and had not had a bath in six months.

God's Kid agreed to take her in providing that they wait a few weeks, so she could recovery from her surgery. Somehow, she would find a way to help her. She had no other options, regardless of her financial or physical situation.

As soon as a plan was worked out, her mother perked up and started packing.

God's Kid and her pregnant daughter, Susan, went to the airport to pick up her mother. She was one of the last to get off the plane. She was shocked and saddened when she saw the frail woman, whose eyes looked dead. It was obvious that her mother tried to put herself together with her last ounce of energy and dignity. The flight attendant looked relieved to have her mother safely into her hands. Her heart ached when she saw her and realized how much she loved this old woman.

Her mother brought two suitcases that contained her only possessions that she needed or cared about. Everything else had been left behind in her Michigan home, that she had lived in for forty years.

God's Kid added a single bed for her in her master bedroom suite. She wanted to be close to her in the event that she needed help. The first thing she did was to give her mother a shower.This is the ultimate gift that a child can give to a parent

Her mother was physically limited and had to use a walker to get around. She loved to eat and was always hungry. God's Kid took her for short drives out of the city and to the ocean. She spoiled her mother as if she was her child and did not deny her many demands.

They shared laughter, mutual respect and acceptance. There were times when it was very hard to love the unlovable. They discussed their differences in religion and spiritual philosophy. She wanted her mother to know that God was not taking notes about what she did or did not do. That God has a special place for her and that she is loved.

God's Kid loved it when she could see her mother's eyes light up. Seeing a smile on her old, tired, wrinkled face and hearing her laughter was heart-warming. There were times when she felt her love. Her mother had not changed she had changed! What a gift it was for her to have the experiences with her mother.

God's Kid was forced to close her office. She was living on her credit cards. She did not have any income and was behind on her house payments. Physically she was deteriorating while her mother's health improved.

Larry sold all of the stuff in their mother's house and rented it out; there was no returning for their mother. Meanwhile their mother got bored and lonely; she would go from chair to chair. She said she was going crazy and became more abusive each day. She tried to ignore her victim role; she never heard her mother say thank-you once! She believed that her children owed her and she was collecting her dues!

God's Kid contacted a home for the elderly to see if she could take her mother in where she can be around people and activities. They told her that if her mother could walk unaided, they would accept her. She took her to the home and showed her around. Her mother set her walker aside and walked across the room on her own.

She thinks that God must have held her up! When they accepted her, she was relieved. God's Kid promised to visit her often and to take her home on weekends.

Wanda came to California from Florida. Together they arranged for their mother to have Medi-Cal, so the State could help pay for their Mother's care. This opened many doors and made it possible for her to pre-register her mother for full care if she needed it.

Her mother kept falling and she had to be taken to the hospital several times. On her last trip to the hospital, she went to visit her and she demanded that they release her. Her mother said that she had not been feed in days and they were making a guinea pig out of her.

God's Kid, found a wheel chair and told her mother that she was going to get her things together so she could leave. When the staff tried to stop her, she reminded them that her mother was ninety years old and that they were killing her.

When she ordered her mother into a wheel chair, her eyes got very big. Once in the hospital elevator as they were leaving, her mother broke out in laughter and could not stop. She had never heard her mother laugh so loud.

She took her mother to her favorite restaurant so she could eat.

Her mother could not return to the independent living and

needed full care. It was time to check into "Plan B." Fortunately, they had a bed and were able to accept her. She made sure that her mother was tucked in.

*****

Her house was in foreclosure and she needed a quick sale. She did not have any idea of what or where she would go. Financially she could not afford to stay in California. She studied a map of the U.S. and eliminated where she did not want to live. She told some of her close friends and children about her dilemma. All she had was her faith to hang onto; she could not trust her head.

She considered going into the ministry for Unity. She contacted a friend in Michigan who was a minister and a man that she loved and spiritually admired. He asked," if there was anything that she wanted to do that, she had not done." He told her that she has a ministry in AA. He asked her to look into the desires of her heart before she makes a commitment to the Unity ministry.

She continued to study the map and Colorado was a state that she had wanted to check out. The more she learned about Colorado the more interested she became, especially with Colorado Springs.

Her house was sold but the buyer backed out. They had to find another buyer fast. An investor bought the house and gave her top dollar. She was planning to make a quick trip to Colorado when she was rushed to the hospital again. Another surgery meant that she was not going anywhere for a while.

She got the Colorado Springs Sunday newspaper and had a good idea of what to expect. She called the real estate Board and asked where the best area in the city was. She was told that the north end was a fast growing preferred area. She contacted a management company and arranged to lease a condominium in Briargate, sight unseen.

She arranged for movers to pick up her furniture and transport it to the condominium in Colorado Springs. While she was packing, she thought about her five ex-husbands who lived near. There was a lot in her past that she did not want to remember, and there was a lot more that she did not want to forget.

It was going to take real courage and letting go for her to make this move.

Her adult children were doing well and busy with their families and careers. She did not hear from them except when they needed a baby sitter. She felt abandoned by them and they felt abandoned by her. She taught them to be responsible and independent. She did not teach them to be sensitive or thoughtful.

Her friends were falling in love and getting on with life. Her Mom was tucked in at the nursing home and getting excellent care. She asked her children to check in on her so she would not feel forgotten. Her mother was aware of her desperate situation and understood. She expressed an interest in going to Colorado with her. She knew that it would be impossible for her to find affordable care in Colorado.

She was emotionally, physically and mentally drained and on empty. She was fighting to survive and spiritually dependent. She was moving into the unknown without support of her friends and family to cling or hide behind. She was full of remorse, regret and grief of what could have been. It was just God and her. When it came time for her to leave, she could not say her good-byes. The separation pain was too intense.

She knew that the women and her children were especially upset with her leaving.

She wrote a God letter and went to the beach. She said the

third step prayer and asked for guidance, protection and direction. She buried the letter deep in the sand and covered it with a rock. She promised God that she would not look back. She had to be totally God reliant.

*****

She asked God for strength that she might achieve
She was made weak that she might learn to obey
She asked God for health that she might do great things
She was given infirmity that she might do better things
She asked for riches that she might be happy
She was given poverty that she might be wise
She asked for power that she might have the praise of women
She was given weakness that she might feel the need of God
She asked for all things that she might enjoy life
She was given life that she might enjoy all things
She got nothing that she asked for but everything that she had hoped for
Author Unknown

CHAPTER 8

Escaping to Colorado

With God buckled into her front seat, God's Kid left for Colorado.

She was a woman on a mission. She could not make the transition without faith that God would do for her what she could not do for herself. The twelve hundred-mile drive to Colorado Springs gave her plenty of time to reflect and process. She believed that God had a plan and the move would not be in vain. There was no turning back.

When she reached the city limits of Colorado Springs, she saw that they were still having winter weather in April. The trees were bare and the landscaping was brown. She had expected to see beautiful green mountains with spring flowers blooming.

She drove to the north of the city to a motel. She was looking forward to resting up before her furniture arrived. She met with the property manager and checked out the condominium that she had rented. She was pleased with the location and condition of her new home.

She had barely laid her head down on the pillow, when she got a call from the movers telling her that they wanted to deliver her furniture the next day. She questioned them about their urgency. She was told that a storm was on its way. How could that be? It was a beautiful sunny day.

She met the movers who quickly unloaded and set up the furniture. A couple hours after they had left, the sky exploded.

The house shook from the rain, thunder and hail. Now she understood what springtime in the Rockies was all about. The storm left her feeling shaken and rattled.

With all the turbulence outside, she kept busy unpacking. She felt like she had really arrived after buying groceries, having her clothes in the closets and her bed made.

A couple days later, there was a terrific windstorm. Mother Nature was giving her quite a welcome.

She began to explore the area. The people were very friendly and kind. She felt comfortable wherever she went. Strangers went out of their way to be helpful and welcomed her; this reminded her of the people in the mid-west.

She had been a square peg trying to fit in a round hole in California. She felt like she belonged in Colorado and that she could be herself.

In California, trust has to be learned and earned. In Colorado, trust was automatic and unconditional. It was a relief to be anonymous and to have a new beginning. She could live by the golden rule without motives, doing unto others, as she would have them do onto her.

Colorado has two seasons, winter and summer. As spring approached, she enjoyed seeing the area come alive. There were the most beautiful rainbows in between the thunderstorms. The snow capped mountains turned green and flowers bloomed with beautiful colors. The robins returned and the birds were singing their hearts out. She loved opening her windows and lying in bed listening to the sounds of nature.

The fresh air filled her lungs and her eyes soaked up the beauty that was around her.

She was aware of being fragile and knew that she had to take it easy. She needed to detox emotionally from the move and her surgeries. She reviewed her priorities and was gentle with herself. She wanted to stand still and do nothing for a while. She thanked God for having such a wonderful place to live.

She continued to venture out into the city so she could become more familiar with the area. The more that she saw, the more she liked. She thanked God everyday for giving her courage to change, even if it was an act of desperation. She felt more at home in Colorado than any other place that she had ever lived.

She wished that her friends and family could be with her. She thought about the quality of life that she saw and what an ideal place to raise a family.

*****

HELLO GOD

I called today to talk awhile
I need a friend who will listen to my anxiety and trial
You see, I cannot quite make it through a day on my own
I need your love to guide me so I will not feel alone
I want to ask you to keep my family safe and sound
To fill their lives with confidence for whatever fate they are bound
Give me the faith to face each hour throughout the day
And not to worry over things I cannot change in any way
Thank-you God for being home and listening to my call
For giving me such good advice when I stumble and fall
Thank-you for being home and listening to my troubles and sorrow
Goodnight God, I love you too and will call again tomorrow
Author Unknown

*****

She scouted the local newspaper for ideas and employment opportunities. Vacation could not last forever and work was inevitable. She did an inventory of her strengths and weakness as an employee. She realized that her greatest weakness was computers. It was obvious that unless she got past that fear, she would be unemployable. She enrolled in computer classes to learn the basics, without a computer at home the class would not help.

She lacked the thirst to learn since leaving the "Nut House." She had a lot of apprehension because of her work history. She had to learn to be an employee.

*****

She promised her daughter, Susan, that she would return to California for her wedding three months after she relocated. When she boarded the flight, she was apprehensive. With all of her "do's and don'ts" it was hard for her to endorse any marriage. She once believed that marriage was a promise of happiness and a guarantee for the future. She had to put aside her own disillusionment and be supportive of her daughter.

Her daughter's wedding was beautifully done in the Catholic Church. She had a large reception after the service, which was also attended by her father. God's Kid was very uncomfortable with the drinking. The grandchildren were out of control, so she gathered them up and took them home. This gave her an excuse to make her escape and to be helpful at the same time.

She was very happy when it came time for her to return to Colorado. On the flight, back she got affirmation that this was where she belonged. It was good to be home!

*****

She became concerned about her savings and paying rent. She was ready to start looking for a home to buy. She contacted a broker who advised her where she should buy. The area was having a housing recession and it was a buyers market. She looked at several homes that were too large. She did not want to live in a condominium and eliminated what she did not want.

She was shown an eight-year-old tri-level home that was a veteran repossession. It was in a good area on a large lot; it had been neglected but not abused. She submitted a low bid that was accepted. It was perfect for her, not too big and not too small. It had a huge master bedroom suite with walk-in closets, a family room with a brick fireplace, a large country kitchen and an oversized two-car garage.

She was happy when the deal closed and she had the keys to the front door. She remained in the condominium while the interior was being completely redone. She wanted the home to be in excellent condition when she moved in.

The dull, dark rooms lightened up with the newly painted walls. She had beautiful mauve carpeting installed that replaced the ugly, dark brown. She had custom drapes made for all the windows that added warmth. She replaced the appliances and flooring and had the outsides of the house painted. It was beautiful when it was finished.

The 9,000 square-foot open yard was a challenge. She hired a man to haul away all the rocks and junk that was in the yard. Then she had two tons of top soil delivered and planted twenty pounds of grass seed.

The home gave her the feeling of permanency and belonging to the community.

The neighbors joined in with her enthusiasm and offered to help. It was obvious that they were delighted in seeing the neglected house getting love and care.

She spent most of her days working in the yard with sweat running down her smiling face. She began to realize that the remorse that she had for so many years was going away and she was happy.

It was humbling to have the concerns and caring of her neighbors. She could not express to them her feelings of joy and happiness. She reassured them that she was fine and kept smiling.

*****

She went to her mailbox one day and found a letter from Larry telling her that their brother, Bob, had died. Apparently, he came home from work and died while sitting in his chair. They thought that he was asleep. He had already been buried when she received the letter.

She had not seen or heard from him since he took baby Caroline back to North Carolina. That was eighteen years ago. Any hope that she could have a relationship with him was history.

She contacted her mother to see if she was all right with losing her son. She did not express any grief or loss. Bob had been very abusive to her too. She told her mother that when she gets to heaven to tell Bob that she forgives him. Her mother responded that he would probably be in the other place.

*****

She began to feel a need to check in with AA. She had to come out of hiding and look for the friends that she has not met. She could be setting herself up unknowingly by avoiding contact with AA.

Regardless of how many years she had, whenever she is in a new area it was almost like starting over. She had to get back to basics and the habits of sobriety by attending meetings. She did not want to make AA her whole life, but a way of life.

*****

She loved the season changes and the beautiful winters in the Rockies. She spent her first Christmas holiday season alone but did not feel alone. She was completely detached from the holiday commercial materialism. She had wanted to skip the holidays for many years so that she could meditate on the real reason for the season. She got a completely new and deeper perspective of the holiday season with this experience.

The day after Christmas, she got a call that her ninety-year-old mother was dying. The nurse told her that she could talk to her mother on the phone. The last thing to leave her body would be her hearing.

A part of her wanted to believe that her mother would live forever. Her mother had lived many lives; she was ready to leave this world. All she could say was that she loved her and encouraged her to go for the light. She reminded her that she had many people waiting for her. God's Kid believes that death is the ultimate spiritual experience!

Her mother's body was sent to Michigan where the family gathered for her funeral. Her mother had spoken often about her demise.

God's Kid had a hard time composing herself at her funeral. She listened to the little old preacher's kind words and found it funny. The entire scene was so surreal with her mother lying in her casket with her watch on and in a green dress. (She hated green) She had a hard time holding back from laughing. She was happy that it was all over for her mother.

She was buried in Detroit next to her parents, brothers and son. She thanked God for the gift of unconditional love and the friendship that they had shared.

*****

She had given up on real estate after having been licensed in California for fifteen years. Her broker's license validated her and was her security for a long time, whether she used it or not. She convinced herself that it is better to be a, "have been, than a has not."

She decided to see if she could get a Colorado brokers licensed. She took the required classes and sent to California Department of Real Estate for verification and status of her license. She studied at home with a Colorado prep book and set a date for the state board exam.

To her delight, she passed the state exam by two points. It felt good knowing that she had not given up her license completely but gained with the Colorado Brokers. This made letting go much easier. She had no idea what she was going to do with it or if she was ever going to put it into use.

She began applying for work with a resume and reference letters in hand. She lacked confidence with what she had to offer an employer. She applied at a temporary agency feeling very unqualified.

It was no longer about wanting to work but if she could find work. She was getting desperate and willing to do anything.

God's Kid was living on the edge and unable to make her house payments again. All she could find was temporary work at a minimum wage. She had to apply for food stamps.

She caught a spiritual flu and got angry with God. She had done everything that she could to find employment and the doors would not open. She questioned God about how much lower would she have to go. She laid face down on the floor with her arms spread, begging for help.

A woman friend of hers from California had moved to Las Vegas and assured her that there was plenty of work there. She used some of the money that her mother had left her and rented out her house. Most of her stuff went to storage. She got a small U-Haul trailer for the items that she wanted to take with her.

She was heart sick about leaving Colorado. She wanted to think that this side trip was temporary and that she could always return.

She had nothing to lose that she had not already lost. She took off for Nevada with bald tires on her car and no insurance, pulling a trailer. She was caught in a blizzard in Utah and almost lost control of her car twice. She was angry with God and with herself.

She was relieved when she got to Ruth's house alive. She agreed to rent her a room in her house that also included her two teenagers. Being a roommate was a new experience for her. She found it very difficult to adjust to the two wild teenagers. She was reminded of her own kids who were out of control when they were teens.

Ruth had a major gambling addiction and would be in the casinos for days. She would return home full of remorse, depressed and suicidal. The insanity had taken over as she continued going back to the casino's, thinking that she could hit the big one.

Fortunately, God's Kid does not have a gambling problem. She has worked too hard for what little she has and does not want to throw it away. She was afraid of the illusion that she has seen with friends who have a gambling problem. This was one healthy fear that she was going to hang onto.

God's Kid could not adjust to the living conditions at Ruth's and realized that the arrangement was not going to work. She found a cheap place in a community that had shared units called commons. She got a temporary job with a property management company in their accounting department. She would return to her little room and at night, the building came alive.

When she went to work in the morning, she could see bodies passed out on the grounds.

Someone who had a key to her unit robbed her. She started to look for a better place after being concerned about her personal safety. She found a nice studio apartment in an older well-managed community.

At times she could visualize herself as being homeless, pushing a cart down the street. She tried in every way that she knew to cut expenses.

She checked the ads for roommates and spoke with a woman called Dee-Dee who was a property manager for a large newer apartment complex. She was offered a job as her assistant and a room in her condominium. She accepted the position and quit her accounting job.

*****

A couple days after God's Kid moved in with Dee, a police officer came to the door asking for her. She thought that something had happened to one of her kids.

She was given a phone number to call in Michigan. When she called, a former sister-in-law told her that her brother, Larry, had died in his sleep the night before.

Her insides exploded, she could not believe that he was gone. He was only forty-seven years old. She had never experienced such awful emotional pain and anguish in all her life.

She called her sister, Wanda, and brother Leonard, who confirmed that he had died from a heart attack. She was paralyzed with grief.

Larry was buried on his birthday, March 1st.

She was alone in Sin City and did not have anyone to grab onto for comfort. She was struggling financially and barely able to buy food for herself. She was trapped and powerless. She could not afford to attend his funeral and doubted if she could have faced the loss.

Her employer refused to give her time off work. She was needed, to collect the rents that were due the first of the month...

She was comforted by the special relationship she had with Larry. She knew that he would be with their mother.

She thanked God for giving her the ability to know real love.

*****

IN THE VALLEYS I GROW

Sometimes life seems hard to bear, full of sorrow, trouble and woe
It is then that I have to remember that it is in the valleys that I grow
If I always stayed on the mountaintop and never experienced pain
I would never appreciate God's love and would be living in vain
I have so much to learn and my growth is very slow
Sometimes I need the mountaintops, but it is in the valleys that I grow
I do not always understand why things happen as they do
I am very sure of one thing; my God will see me through
Forgive me God for complaining when I am feeling so very low
Just give me a gentle reminder that it is in the valleys that I grow
Continue to strengthen me God and use my life each day
To share your love with others and help them find their way
Thank you for the valleys, one thing I know
The mountaintops are glorious, but it is in the valleys that I grow
Author Unknown

*****

She started to act out on her pain by getting into some destructive behavior. She would hang out in the casinos to eat, listen to music and check out the men. She was seeking relief and developing a very dangerous, "I don't care attitude." She began feeling resentful toward everyone who crossed her path. The woman that she lived and worked with was on drugs.

She later learned that the job she had was only temporary. The other assistant manager was on pregnancy leave and due to return soon.

She was nine years sober and had hit another bottom. She felt as if she was not going to be able to get out of this one.

She had met an old gal who went by the name of "Nevada Red." She took her under her wing and breathed love and hope into her broken heart.

She helped her to take the 11th-step through the "Prayer of Saint Francis." This prayer expressed how she could see, feel and wish to be. She took each line of the prayer and incorporated it into her life. She was told to take each sentence of the prayer as a step.

*****

Step 1. Make me a channel of they peace, that where there is hatred, I may bring love.

Step 2. Where there is a wrong, may I bring the spirit of forgiveness?

Step 3. Where there is discord, may I bring harmony?

Step 4. Where there is error, may I bring truth?

Step 5. Where there is doubt, may I bring faith?

Step 6. Where there is despair, may I bring hope?

Step 7. Where there are shadows, may I bring light?

Step 8. Where there is sadness, may I bring joy?

Step 9. May I seek to comfort rather than to be comforted?

Step 10. To understand rather than to be understood?

Step 11. To love rather than to be loved?
Step 12. To forgive rather than to be forgiven?

She could chose how she wanted to live, with hatred, discord, error, doubt, despair, or sadness. Or she could live with love, forgiveness, harmony, truth, faith, hope, and joy. It was up to her.

*****

She chose to leave Las Vegas and return to Colorado Spring

It was no longer important what she believed, as long as she kept the faith.

She sold her stereo TV so that she could buy some tires for her car and arranged to return to Colorado.

She could not to move back into her home because of the lease. She stayed with a friend until she could get an apartment.

She had become a professional job seeker.

She got a call for a position as a Property Manager for a 333-unit luxury apartment community. They offered her a good salary and a free apartment. She brought her furniture out of storage and moved into a beautiful apartment that had a great view of Pikes Peak and the Front Range.

The first month on the job, she increased the revenue by $35,000. The tenants were dealing and the employees were stealing. She got accountability and found herself in crises management. She put in many long hours and quickly discovered that this was not going to be a popularity contest. It took her six months to get rid of the crime. She had to update the leases so she would know who was living where. She had a new dedicated staff that was honest and hard working. Their reputation as a community improved and there were people waiting for a vacancy.

The apartments were in foreclosure and owned by the government. She was informed that the community had been sold to an investment group. She was confident that her dedication and performance would be an asset to the new owners. She was laid off after being there for a year so they could bring in their own management team. She was very disappointed with their decision.

She continued to live in the community until the lease on her home was up. She was given excellent references and able to draw unemployment. She rented out the second bedroom in her apartment.

She began to think that life was an endurance contest. She was happy when the day came for her to move back into her home. She had it repainted and cleaned before she moved in her furniture.

It took every ounce of her energy to move her stuff again. She was hurting physically from all the packing and unpacking. She swore to herself that after eight moves this was going to be her last. She had hit bottom and needed stability in her life. It felt wonderful to be home!

It was getting easier for her to find work. She was offered a management position at a large problem apartment's community. There was a lot of deferred maintenance and hostile tenants. A couple of buildings was not suitable for life and had been taken over by cockroaches. Fifty units were leased by the mentally challenged. She was put on a limited budget and under staffed. She was paid well for the work, but questioned if it was really worth it.

She called in drug enforcement and had an undercover officer move onto the property. She had her life threatened and was afraid to drive home alone at night.

She was laid off so they could hire a man. She later learned that they regretted their decision and wished that they had kept her on. They said that they should have hired a maintenance supervisor to help her instead.

She was given excellent references from her employer. She had collected a portfolio of references and a wealth of experience. She did not want to be married to her work and began to think that property management may not be for her.

She wanted a job with benefits and not a career. She wanted to be able to leave her work behind when she finished the day.

A large mail order company was looking for seasonal help. She had submitted three applications before she was called in for an interview for their customer service department. She was hired at $5.85 an hour without benefits and had three weeks of intensive training. She spent her days wearing a headset that was plugged into the phones and staring at a computer. She worked in a dark basement with two hundred other representatives. She was a worker among workers.

Her sponsor/mentor had told her to pray for sobriety, sanity, surrender, safety, sweetness and serenity. She realizes that she had to be careful about what she asked for in prayer. God does answer prayers. There was no doubt that this job would be the ultimate test in patience and sweetness.

Many times, she wanted to tell the customers off and had to bite her tongue. This job was very demanding and disciplining her in areas that she never expected. The majority of the customers that she spoke to were very kind and co-operative when she helped them. The customers, who were intimidating and rude, usually wanted something for nothing.

Mentally she would travel the U.S. while on the phones with the customers. When customers upset her, she would have to go to the bathroom.

It was very hard for her to turn the other cheek while being verbally abused. She had to remind herself not to take it so personally, even when she knew that the customers were lying. The company policy was that the customer is always right, in spite of what she thought.

When the holiday rush was over, she would be out of work again, unless she could get a job in their checks division.

She begged them to transfer her. Thank God, she was hired with full benefits.

She earned extra money by renting out a room in her house. She was determined to stay on the job, no matter what. She volunteered for overtime whenever it was available. She was relieved to have benefits and a better work environment. The customers were easier to work with.

She kept her distance from the politics and learned to swim with the sharks. She saw contradictions caused by the company's many growing pains. Employees were abusing the customers and each other. They were still operating as they had ten years before. It was hard for her to avoid giving advice or opinions.

She preferred to work the afternoon shift for the extra pay. There was a lot of hanky-panky going on around her. Security was very poor, an open invitation for theft and embezzlement. There was a 75% turn around with the new hires. Every three months they would have a new supervisor. It did not take long for her to gain seniority.

They finally hired someone who knew something about management. She began to notice some positive changes and uniformity. The company was open to solutions. They listened to her suggestions and at times acted on them.

Security was a major concern. They started to do background checks on all the employees. When the results came back, people started to disappear.

She worked for two years without missing a day of work.

She was able to set up a small 401K and make some improvements to her home. She continued to subsidize herself with roommates. She was able to buy a few extras for herself and took a paid vacation to California.

Her world got very small; she would go from work to home and home to work. She felt content with the simplicity in her life. She was healing emotionally and spiritually.

She began to realize that her exact nature was changing. She was softer and sweeter. She had not had a crisis in a few years. She planted her garden and enjoyed watching it grow.

She continued to attend AA meetings. She was not involved with the people because her work kept her drained most of the time. Showing up was the best that she could do. Her personal contact with God was consistent and strong.

She was able to sneak calls to her children from work. She was very proud of how well they were doing. There were times when she missed them very much and ached for their closeness.

In her absence, the children's father took a special interest in the grandchildren and made them his life. There were times when she resented the help that he was giving to them. She was struggling and he was very secure financially.

*****

God's Kid got a phone call from her daughter, Becky, who was living in Virginia. She told her that she was wanting out of her marriage. They spoke, mother to daughter and daughter to mother for the first time in years. They talked about Becky's feelings and concerns.

Her husband was in the Navy and scheduled to be shipped over seas. Becky did not want to stay in Virginia or California.

God's Kid has vowed to stay completely out of her children's relationship problems. She was the last person who could advise them in that area.

She had prayed for the day when her children could join her in Colorado. Nothing would make her happier than to have Becky living near and being in her grandchildren's lives.

She had never met her granddaughter Brooke, who was two years old. It had been many years since she had seen Becky's oldest daughter, Adrienne, who was in high school.

They were strangers with so many years and miles between them. She was thrilled with a second chance to resolve their differences.

She agreed to help Becky and the children until they found a home. Their life styles are very different; she discussed the guidelines and the importance of working together. She believed that they had an understanding. She was anxious and looking forward to the day that they would be together.

Shortly before Becky left Virginia, she told her that she was pregnant with a third child. She was also dealing with some major health problems. This came as a surprise; she was concerned about her separating from her husband with a new baby on the way.

Becky arrived as planned. When she came home from work, Becky and her family were sitting on her front porch. Her heart almost burst when she saw their smiling faces and the children greeted her with hugs. Hearing them say, Grandma was music to her ears.

God's Kid moved a roommate out so she could make room for Becky and the children. Her focus was on their needs and familiarizing them with the area. She had not thought about their need to relax after being on the road for days. They did not appreciate her giving them a tour of the area.

She explained to Becky that she was financially limited and was willing to give what she could. She would need her help with expenses. She tried to communicate to Becky about compromise and compatibility in their living arrangement. She was ignored and realized that Becky was not flexible or cooperating.

Her requests were invalidated and Becky became very defiant. She was verbally abusive toward her children and her. She was living with insanity in her own home.

She prayed that once Becky was settled and comfortable, that the mood swings would even out.

A week after Becky arrived, a moving van pulled up to drop off some of her stuff before they took what remained to storage. She asked Becky to work with her because of the limited amount of room. Becky filled half of the garage and packed the rooms. It was almost impossible to move around the house. She felt imposed upon with all of Becky's stuff. She sat on the couch and cried.

When she returned home from work, she would find the house trashed. There was food all over the place. If she said anything to Becky, she would blow up and twist around what she had said. She was forced to retreat to her bedroom and isolate herself.

She became afraid when she saw the hatred in Becky's eyes. There were times when she was concerned about what she might do to her.

She reaffirmed to herself that she would not allow anyone, including her own child to abuse her emotionally or mentally, regardless of what she had to do, even if it meant throwing her pregnant daughter and her grandchildren out.

She could not ignore how mentally and verbally abusive she was. She told her to leave, knowing that her father had bought her a home. Becky found some people to move her stuff. She left without a thank-you, leaving God's Kids home, filthy and trashed...

She later heard that she had a baby boy. She did not see or

hear from Becky for over two years after she moved out. For a long time it hurt that, it did not work out between them. Her heart ached for the relationship that she wanted with Becky. They were so close, but so far apart!

✸✸✸✸✸

She had days when her workload was too much. She was feeling stressed with all the job pressures and poor morale. She tried to fake it and hoping she could make it. Her days as a super achiever and one of their top producers were getting the best of her.

Her patience was giving away and she started to think about a change. Her health was getting her attention; she knew that her clock was ticking.

She missed her children and grandchildren in California. She wanted family in her life.

She began thinking about the day when God would call her home. She did not want to have any regrets when her time came. She knew that she was not going to get out of this life alive.

She had walked the walk emotionally naked in most areas of her life. She had been forced to defend her character on several occasions. She had to maintain her faith and dignity even when she was walking on fire. She had been to war with egos, including hers and choked on pride only to fall back on her knees. She keeps asking God, "What's it all about?"

She never thought that she would be grateful for what she had to let go. She was grateful for the courage to say, "No thank-you" and being in touch with her limitations. She can be more confident with her choices and the affirmation she receives.

She had chosen to remain emotionally unattached from serious intimate relationships, while she strived to be the person that she wanted to be...

She had enjoyed her independence and freedom in spite of all the hardships that she has experienced. She is less self-reliant and more God reliant with every challenge or change. Developing faith is quite a process!

God has given her big eyes, new ears and a new heart!

She put her beautiful house up for sale and prepared to return to California. She asked top dollar and signed a ninety-day contract. After the listing expired, she found another real estate broker and reduced the price. He was confident that he could sell the house and told her to start packing. She joined in with the optimistic Broker and started to sort, sell and pack.

Another ninety days had passed and she was living out of boxes. The agent tried every marketing technique that he knew and still did not come up with a buyer. She saw herself in the faces of the real estate agents that did come by. She noted their lack of professionalism and wanted to say, "Don't you know who I am?" Been there, did that!

She had let down her California family and friends who were anxiously waiting for her return.

She had to look at her motives behind her wanting to relocate. When she got honest with herself, it was clear that she wanted to escape from the loneliness, physical concerns and the stress from her work.

She unpacked her will and surrendered! She had forgotten why she moved to Colorado in the first place. A smile came to her face as she unpacked. The experience took care of her urges to move.

God wanted to remind her that He was in control. She needed to keep listening and learning when God says, "no."

She put her house back together and embraced her surroundings. She realized that she had done a major job of a house cleaning! Over the years, she has cleaned the closets, attic, basements and of her life. The ghost and garbage was long gone.

She discovered that she could not buy love at K-Mart. She made room for many spiritual gifts and could see what she could not see before. Life gave her hugs and smiles.

Her home was more than just a piece of real estate. She loved her wholesome environment that she lives in. God is her landlord.

*****

She returned to California for a visit, she saw desperation on her friend's faces that were without guidance or a mentor. She heard their cries and knew that she could not be their savior. She was in touch with how powerless she was and that she could not play God. It was very humbling when she was told how much she was needed. She left feeling sad.

She had been sober longer than she was drunk and was aware that there are no guarantees. As long as she keeps doing what she is doing, one day at a time, there is a real good chance that she will die sober.

She was told that if she were willing to be willing to go to any length no matter what, her life would make a 180-degree change. Many times, she felt like she was spinning in circles, until she learned that it was part of the process.

She will never forget the days when she kicked and screamed asking, "What's it all about." She has learned to stand still and wait for it to pass; meanwhile, she would exercise her spiritual muscle.

There has been a major shift in her thinking over the years. What she once thought was important does not matter anymore. She can look in the mirror and smile back at the face that she sees. She is truly a woman who has been born again.

She needed every lonely moment to develop a relationship with herself. She has learned to be a real friend and is comfortable with God, herself and others.

It has been by the grace of God that she was able to detox from men and not prostitute herself out of loneliness. She can see how illusions and false reality can be deceiving. It is so easy to get on the wrong road without the wisdom to know better.

It was very hard to have close relationships when fear is in control. She has learned to love more and demand less without expectations. What a freedom, when the fear is replaced with faith.

Fear did not leave over night. (F-E-A-R) Fear is false expectations appearing real or faces everything and recover.

Recovery is a very long process that can take many years and will continue as long as she is still above ground.

It is impossible to have emotional sobriety without spiritual sobriety. She had to give time, time and more time before there was any balance.

It is hard to love when you are not feeling loveable. It is easy to be hooked on the feeling, only to learn that feelings are not fact and that love is not a feeling. Love is an emotion and action.

Trust and discernment are gifts that come with spiritual maturity and the wisdom to know the difference. The more we trust ourselves, the more we can trust others.

Each person, good or bad, has been her teacher. She thanks God for giving her the courage to keep walking the walk. She thanks God for her new heart so she can love unconditionally.

She once commented at work about her simple boring life with simple problems. She did not have any crises to report and everything in her life was good. The co-workers could not relate, they told her that she had what they were seeking. Sometimes she forgets that the search is over and that she is enjoying the journey.

She continued to show up at work for the paycheck. She

was wearing her experiences and challenges like an old pair of comfortable slippers.

She made a conscious effort to have more fun with the customers that she spoke to daily. She took an interest in her co-workers and told them a little bit about herself. She was careful not to say too much to them. She was beginning to like her work, her supervisor and the company. There was a big change in her attitude, instead of being apart from; she was a part of the team.

❊❊❊❊❊

Dear Child of Mine,
As you go through this day, know that I am gently protecting you
I am as near to you as your very breath, as close to you as your heartbeat
I can see the fragile state of your emotions
I know how close to the surface your tender feelings are
I am aware that the wick of your spirit's inner light is flickering in the winds
of your dilemma
You are my child and I am on your side today
I will not allow the flame of your spirit to be snuffed out
I will stand between you and the wind
I will hold you in my love until you are strong again
Do not be troubled or afraid
Do not strive in your own strength, but lean into my love
Be strengthened by my spirit
Find comfort in my mercy
Your Higher Power
Author Unknown

CHAPTER 9

Acceptance and Love

One evening while at work, God's Kid began having numbness in her left arm and the left side of her face. She realized that she might have a problem, so she struggled to the nurse's station for help. An ambulance was called and she was taken to the hospital.

While in route to the emergency room, she was given oxygen and was asked some questions. She had difficulty talking and her thinker was broken. She was kept in the hospital for a couple days while they ran tests.

She had a new HMO doctor who did not seem very happy about having her as a new patient. He was not interested in her medical problem and was reluctant to help her.

She had a friend stop by the hospital and she gave him the key to her house. She needed some clothes and clean underwear. She called a neighbor to let her know that she was in the hospital and asked her to keep an eye on her house.

She was hesitant about contacting her children; she did not want to alarm them. Her daughter, Susan, who worked for a hospital in California, took charge of her mother's care. She told the hospital staff not to give her mother any drugs.

A mystery lady stayed in her room and sat near her bed for hours. She thought that it must have been one of God's angels.

She later learned that her cholesterol was 300 and that she had very high blood pressure. When she returned home, she was dragging her left leg, slurring and drooling. She had a problem with short-term memory and felt detached; some of her memory had been erased.

She could not accept that she was broken and denied that she had a problem. When she went to her doctors for a check-up, he told her to look in the mirror. He said, "Look you had a stroke!" She pushed up her fallen cheek.

Her thoughts would flash back to the 1960s when she lived in Michigan and her children were small. It seemed like the events had happened yesterday. She enjoyed the memories and knew that her brain was playing tricks on her.

She would get lost on the way to the store and could not remember how to get back home. She made a game out of getting lost, until her memory kicked back in.

The stroke scared her and she thought about how her life can change in an instant. With her family history of heart disease and strokes, there was a good possibility that she could die young.

She was encouraged by her friends to write for therapy. There was a lot of her life that she did not want to forget. When she had her thoughts on paper, she could read about herself in the event that she had another stroke.

She has been blessed with so many beautiful friends who have watched her "walk the walk." She was once told that she had a story to share and that it was important to give back what she has been so richly given...

God's Kid had made plans for a trip to Michigan and Virginia with a woman who she worked with. They had been looking forward to the vacation for months before she had her stroke. She knew that she should not travel so soon after a stroke, but; she did not want to disappoint her friend.

When she told her doctor about the trip, he advised against

her going. She decided to go anyway. She felt an urgency to get away before it was too late for her to go anywhere.

They covered many miles. She checked in on her brother, Larry, and her mother's gravesites in Michigan to make sure that they were tucked in. It was very hard for her to see where Larry was buried. This was the first time that she had seen the family plot where her grandparents, brother Jack and mother were buried in Detroit.

She discovered that her brother, Jack, did not have a grave marker. She mentioned this to her brother, Leonard, and sister Wanda; they arranged to have a marker installed.

God's Kid and her friend stopped at Niagara Falls on their way to Arlington, Virginia to visit with her brother Leonard. They drove around Washington D.C. to check it out and visited George at Mount Vernon. She did not have much fun and tired easily.

Once back home she continued to struggle physically. She contacted her doctor and he refused to see her since she went against his orders. She had to find a new HMO doctor fast. She got lucky and found a real doctor who was interested in helping her.

She returned to work six weeks after her stroke. She was still having physical and memory problems. It was either the power of God or her ignorance that made it possible for her to show up for work.

She had to take God's message seriously; she had once again been given a reprieve. It was quite a challenge for her to pretend that she was well when she really was not. She needed to take a good look again at her possible immortality.

She had fleeting thoughts about returning to California. The winter had been especially bad. On one occasion, they had six-foot snowdrifts. The maintenance of her home was almost too much for her at times. Her neighbor told her that he expected to find her laid out in the yard dead one day. He offered to buy her a lawn mower.

She wanted to be closer to her family for all the right reasons. Not for what she wanted or could take from them emotionally, but for what she could give of herself. She had to respect their grandfather and stay in the background. He had been their anchor for a long time and an outstanding grandfather. She knew that her approach would have to be subtle and sincere.

She had lived in Colorado Springs for almost ten years. There was so much that she loved about the area. She was living day-by-day, doing the very best that she could at work and at home.

She gave up on questioning God and was able to accept just about everything that came her way. She was dependent upon prayer and meditation (listening). Weeks would go by and all she got from God was silence. She took this as being a good sign; she was exactly where she was supposed to be. It seemed strange to her that she was not going, doing, needing or wanting. She was content.

She prayed for guidance. She felt that she needed to take care of some unfinished business in Colorado. She was very private, resting in God's arms with a cocoon around her. Her only concern was her health.

She had a wonderful AA home group that included some very special people. She did not attend many meetings, but when she did show up, she always got more than she gave from her group.

She concluded that she might be working for the same company for several more years before she could retire. There were times when she wondered, how much longer she could endure physically. Her energy was gradually being depleted. She knew that she had to maintain a good attitude and look beyond just getting a paycheck. She needed to stop being so darn indifferent.

The management had an attitude change that encouraged her to follow suit. They were under a lot more pressure than she was.

She learned about a co-worker who had a serious drinking problem. She reached out to her and shared some of her experiences with the bottle. She found out what meeting she was attending after work and made an effort to show up to support her. It was not long after that; word must have gotten out at work about her being in AA.

The girls who worked around her started to share confidences. She noticed that they were showing her a new kind of respect, she felt very humbled with their attention. She became more a part of the team at work and less antisocial.

One of the character defects that haunted God's Kid was her problem with blending or mixing socially. Her indifference gave the impression that she was not interested.

She worked with many women and was ashamed about not acknowledging them. They knew so little about each other. She concluded that she would like to get to know them. When she reached out, she met some very special souls.

She had learned that her indifference could only cause separation. She did not realize this about herself when it was happening. Now that she has been able to put a name to it, she had to claim it and do what she could to change it. Change can sometimes be very hard for her. .

✵✵✵✵✵

She arranged to visit her sister, Wanda, in Florida. She had not been to her home since she retired over twenty years ago. It had been over ten years since she had last seen her. They had become distant, she prayed for an opportunity to get to know her.

When the day came for her to leave for Florida, she was at peace. An elderly co-worker took her to the airport and shared with her some of her heartache. She said a prayer for her and made a mental note to reach out to her when she got back.

Flying alone to Florida was a first for her; she had to change flights at the Atlanta Airport. She took a couple deep breaths at Atlanta before she jumped on a train in the airport that would take her to her connecting gate. She arrived in Fort Myers and was relieved when she saw her sister at the bottom of the escalator.

Their week's visit went by fast. She met many of Wanda's friends, visited the sites, walked the beach, went to church and shared. Wanda took her into her world, just as she had done when she was a child. She was amazed at how alive and active Wanda was for being almost eighty-three years old.

God's Kid met an elderly cousin who she had not seen since she was a teenager. Before leaving, she gave Wanda a copy of her book manuscript that she had been working on. She felt like the gap between them was closed. She arrived home she felt good about her visit.

She continued having a hard time physically, and difficulty making it through the day. She could feel herself wilting after being at the desk for just a couple of hours. There were days when her head felt heavy and she had to use her hands to hold her head up. After a day of work, she would return home suffering from pain and problems with circulation....

She contacted her doctor and discovered that her thyroid

was way off. After taking medication, she could feel some of the stress and weakness leave. Her doctor wrote a prescription to her employer requesting that they put her on a thirty-two-hour workweek, with three continuous days off because of hypertension. She was pleased when she heard that she would qualify for short-term disability pay for the extra day off.

Her days as super woman were almost over. She had hoped that the shorter workweek would make a physical difference. She did not want to admit to her limitations, even when she would fall into her bed exhausted every night.

A couple weeks after she returned from Florida, she got a call from Wanda saying that she wanted to visit her in Colorado. She was afraid that the copy of her manuscript had opened Pandora's Box. The last thing that she wanted to do was to offend her.

Wanda usually stays very close to her home in Naples. She was happy that her sister was coming to her home for a visit. She asked her if she had read the manuscript. In a sweet, soft voice that sounded sad and concerned, she asked Barbara if she could have done anything differently. She reassured her that she had done more than she realized. Like herself, she too was a product of a dysfunctional home. They wore similar slippers.

She explained to her that there was not any malice in her heart and that she was okay. Wanda agreed, "Yes, you are okay now." Thank God", she understood!

When Wanda arrived in Colorado, they were having rain showers. After stopping at her house, they went to the beautiful Garden of the Gods. The garden is a special place where God's Kid visits often to meditate. While they were out, they stopped by her work so that she could show her inside to her cubical.

Wanda was her hostage.

When God's Kid is in her car driving, she can be spiritually inspired; she believes it is because God is in the car with to her. Sometimes she thinks that God lives in her car. It is easier for her to share from the heart when she is driving through the mountains.

Being together with her sister was an important chapter in her life. They were friends who lived in two different worlds. They closed the distance between them.

*****

She got back into her routine and continued to feel as if a part of her was dying; the tasks that use to be easy were getting harder. She was frustrated, not knowing the cause or having any solutions. She spent her weekends resting and had to neglect some of her chores. Her doctor insisted that all the tests came back negative and he did not give a medical explanation for her exhaustion.

She was self-obsessing too much and needed to get out of herself. She had been hibernating and putting on a happy face, pretending.

One evening, God's Kid invited her co-workers from the afternoon shift over for a tamale dinner after work. One of the women in her department made Mexican rice. She was surprised and happy when about forty co-workers showed up.

A friend mentioned to God's Kid that their AA home group needed her help. The meeting room had been neglected and no one was taking care of it. She got the groups permission to do what she could. She sorted and trashed the junk that had been accumulating for years. She had a paint party to cover the dingy, dirty walls. Once it was clean and painted, word got out about the improvements. The group's enthusiasm and help was overwhelming.

They became the largest group in Colorado, who made the

largest contribution to their service office in the area. They followed the guidelines set by AA, the Big Book, and the spiritual principles of the 12 traditions and 12-steps. Most importantly, they had unity and love for every person who entered the room. There we no strangers, they would go the extra mile for each other.

There was no doubt that God was doing for "Walk the Talk" what they could not do for by themselves. The power of example and identification was very strong among them.

God's Kid would go to the meeting room several nights a week after work to clean. She was also their treasurer and made bank deposits for them. While alone in the room, she would have a private meeting with God, thanking him for taking care of His kids.

They had their first annual BBQ and round up. It was successful in bringing them together socially with their families.

She did not think about her aches and pains so much. She smiled when she observed how God was working through and for them.

She celebrated five years of working for the same employer. Very few employees in her department remained over a year. The staff gave her big party with cake, gifts and a certificate. She was humbled when her co-workers expressed their respect, love and sincerity in her accomplishment.

What a victory, being friends with people who suffer in silence at their job like herself. If they only knew, what she was really thinking or what it took for her to keep showing up every day.

She could not hold back the tears of appreciation for their support and love. When she saw the similarities, she realized that she was not so unique. This was one of the greatest growing experiences of in her life, working with these people and for this company.

She loved the unlovable and was able to accept people for exactly who they were, what they were and where they were at in life. Been there, done that!

The prayer of Saint Francis was working in her life. She was emotionally free. Her heart was full of love and void of anger, hurt and resentments.

Her boss was a jerk. She saw him change into a caring team leader, a man that she understood and respected. Once her blinders were lifted, she could see that he was just doing his job. Her self-centeredness made her blind to what was really going on.

At the day's end, she would leave work in pain with a smile on her face.

She celebrated another year of sobriety and her second life. A new friend from California brought her a birthday cake. In Colorado, they do not celebrate birthdays, as they do in California. She missed hearing the group singing Happy Birthday, to her. On this day, they shared by singing. She could see love in their smiling faces.

She was choked up and had a hard time-sharing what was in her heart. She loved the people at "Walk the Talk" so much!

She took the candles from her cake and gave them away to newcomers and people who had less than one year of sobriety. This celebration was for them all.

She will never forget her first candle and first cake. When she would see others who had a lot of year's blowing out a blaze of candles, she could not imagine seeing herself as a long timer. The one-day-at-a-time, does add up, if she does not drink or die.

She give all credit to her God for each day and knows that it has been a "we" thing. She could not help but think of the many people who we have lost to this disease and the insanity of addiction.

Their founder, Bill Wilson, once said that if he were to change anything, he would change the slogan "keep coming back" to ", *STAY.*" Unfortunately, many do not stay long enough to find out what the AA life is really like. If only they could see ahead and what a wonderful life, they can have by just not drinking, one day at a time.

She thinks often about her adult children and the 1200 miles that separate them. She keeps close phone contact with them, but feels detached. When she thinks about her grand-children, they are beautiful faces in a picture. She does not know them! They too have found her to be a distant voice. She was unsure about how much of herself that she wants to give to her family. She had emotionally distances herself from them.

*****

She got a call from a woman friend in California who was having some serious personal problems and needed her help. She had her promise that she would not do anything stupid and en-couraged her to come to Colorado.

She agreed to fly to Colorado so that they could get down to what was really going on with her. When the woman arrived, she looked like she had been through a wringer. Her lights were out and her face was frozen. She was disorientated and her thinking was scrambled.

She was desperate and willing to find solutions. God's Kid did not know what to do with her, so she put in an urgent call to God for help.

She felt so powerless to help this friend. She was suicidal, mentally and spiritually in trouble. Her faith was gone and she was angry with God. She could identify with what she was ex-periencing.

She once asked her mentor/sponsor, "Why do we have to

struggle so much?" She was told, "So our experiences could help others." This statement went flying way over her head at the time. Now she knows what she meant.

God's Kid had known this woman for thirteen years and has seen her walk on fire and not drink. She shared what happened to her and what she had to do to get past it. The more we shared, the clearer the solution became.

The first thing that she told her was to stop praying. Her knees must have hurt from praying so much. She had tried to manipulate God into doing for her what she could not do for herself and it was not working. They agreed that it was unrealistic to try to figure out God. To know who God is, all we need to do is to look at the miracles around us.

After having been on a spiritual path for many years, it is not important what our personal concept of God is. As stated with, "I am what I am." God can be very elusive. When she loosens up her grip on God, she can breathe easier.

Her friend looked at her with shock but agreed to let go of prayer, for a while.

Sometimes her God talk was just pretty words and nothing more than babbling. The purest prayer can be a thought of gratitude. A simple prayer can be a thank-you.

God's Kid was either simple-minded or just content with spiritual ignorance. The more she tries to figure out what God's job is, the more she is trying to manipulate.

She has walked hand in hand with her Higher Power, boogying through life. When her God was small or on vacation, it was because she is trying to be in control and not taking time to listen. Sometimes God whispers to her when she wants Him to scream. God can get so small he disappears, poof!

Each day when she lets go and gives her WILL to God, she is more trusting of the results. She has learned that God's will for her is perfection. She reminds herself again that, God does not wear a watch and what will be, will be.

Meditation is oxygen for the soul. It is hard for her to meditate when she is in the unknown. She has to keep her ears open. Intuitively, we do learn how to handle situations that used to baffle us.

The healing steps can be found in the fifth, sixth, seventh, eighth and ninth steps. While in the healing process, she can commune with the spirit and it transcends her nature. She found freedom when the steps worked her, and when she took action, even when she did not want to. She is still willing to be willing to go to any length, no matter what.

She cannot stress enough how very important the healing steps are for a contented sober life. She wishes that she could reach into the hearts of her AA family and hold their hand while they are walking the walk.

Do not give up until you have experienced at least fifty or more miracles in your life.

She discovered that, she has made many subtle changes in her personality, nature, thinking, actions, wisdom, honesty and love. Sometimes she wants more until she realizes that she already has it.

Recovery can be full of contradictions, giving us many choices or escapes. That is when the 12-steps help us to sort things out. She would not be happy, joyous and free if it was not for the help that she got from her sponsor and mentor. God definitely worked through people!

Please do not confuse religion with spirituality. We are not human trying to get spiritual, we are spiritual trying to be human.

God's Kid is not religious she is a spiritual...

She remembers hearing about the Holly Ghost and thought

it was God's spy. She believes that the gift of the spirit we find in recovery is one and the same.

The beauty of AA is that, whatever you do or do not believe, you can personalize or change it. God has nothing to prove and we do not have anything to prove to God. He does not take notes.

*****

She contacted a real estate friend to find out what was going on in the housing market. He was the same optimistic Broker, who encouraged her to pack a couple of years earlier.

She had done a lot of work to her home and wanted his estimate of value. When he arrived, he told her that the market was active and that he would not have any problems selling her home for the price that she wanted.

She signed a listing agreement expecting no results. This time, she was not going to pack until she knew for sure that it was sold. She shocked herself, when she realized that she had just put her home up for sale. She thought what if he was able to find a buyer.

She just wanted to test the market and held back on any expectations.

She did not say anything to her family or friends in California about her house being up for sale again. She was free from motives or issues to stay or go. She knew that she would have to let go of her home eventually, it had become too much for her to take care of.

She definitely did not want to say anything to anyone at work.

Her home was getting a lot of attention from possible buyers. One couple who looked at the house kept driving around the block. Her friend told her that the people were going to buy the home; she realized that she was probably right.

Sure enough, the folks came in with a full price offer and wanted to move in within thirty days. She accepted their offer. She did not get excited because she knew that a lot could go wrong with the deal.

God's Kid avoided thinking about what was going on with the house. It was spring and she had a lot of yard work that needed to be done. She raked ten large bags of leaves that had fallen in the fall. She planted six climbing rose bushes near the back fence.

When she had dirt on her hands, she felt closer to God.

Her health kept getting her attention. Her eyes were hemorrhaging, she had excessive perspiration and her blood pressure was getting out of control. Her days of working were numbered.

She waited for God to say, "No." The realtor encouraged her to start packing and reminded her that the buyers wanted quick possession. She began to think that God had said, "Yes."

It was time for her to get into action and prepare to wrap up ten years of her life in a couple of weeks.

She would have to start telling people she loved "good-bye." She wanted to sneak out of the city and disappear into the sunset; she also knew this would be selfish of her. She remembered the tears from her women friends when she moved out of California and how abandoned they felt.

She had to be spiritually focused and emotionally balanced to walk the walk, knowing that she was not alone.

She felt fragmented, with her head and heart going in two directions at once. She had planted her roots deep. She cared about so many people.

She told her boss that she had sold her home and was returning to California. Her employers and co-workers did not believe that she was leaving, even after she gave her two weeks notice. She had to reassure them that she was serious about leaving.

Memorial Day was coming up and she wanted to work her last day after the holiday. She did not want to be in the heavy traffic. She arranged for the movers to pick up her furniture and deliver it to storage in California.

She told her friends at "Walk the Talk" that she was going to be leaving at the end of the month. They responded with overwhelming love. It was very humbling to hear how much they were going to miss her and their expressions of gratitude for what she had done. She was speechless and choked up with emotions, their love brought tears.

After some frantic insistence from the realtor, she began packing, sorting and giving stuff away to the girls at work. It became obvious to them that she was moving.

She was also leaving her daughter, Becky, and three grand children in Colorado Springs.

✳✳✳✳✳

God's Kid's daughter, Becky, is very sick with multiple addictions; they had been estranged on and off for several years. She had to release her with tough love. Becky's two youngest Brooke and Jeremy are very special to her.

While she was packing, Becky's daughter and her oldest granddaughter, Adrienne, came to her door asking for help. She had left home after a major fight with her mother. She was a senior in high school and had plans to attend the University of Colorado in the fall. She wanted her freedom and time with her grandmother.

Adrienne arranged to stay with friends after her grandmother moved...

✳✳✳✳✳

Her co-workers gave her a going away party and a Bronco's shirt. She did not realize how much she would be missed at work. The love and sincerity that her friends expressed was real.

She was given another wonderful reference letter and many hugs. On her final day of work, it was hard for her to sit still and work at her desk. Her furniture had been picked up and her car was in the parking lot loaded with her stuff.

She tried not to think and kept on working. She swore that she would never have another head set stuck in her ear again. The department manager came to her desk and told her that she could leave early. She could not get out of there fast enough.

Her boss asked her if he could walk her to the door and she declined. She had walked in alone and wanted to walk out alone. God had said, "YES."

CHAPTER 10

Family and Retirement

As she drove away from Colorado Springs, she did not want to look back at the city that she had come to love so much. She wanted to enjoy the silence and to take it one mile at a time. This was another trip into the unknown. Strangely, she felt a calm and inner-peace. She was going to and not running away.

She felt concern with her lack of separation pain. She was confident and comfortable with what she may find down the road. She expected that the emotions she had stuffed would surface later.

She took mental pictures of the beautiful landscape as she was driving. She knew that she had to stay in the moment. When she stopped in Arizona, she embraced the warm air for the first time in months...

She tensed up when she reached California's state line. She said a quick prayer as the cars whizzing past her going eighty miles per hour. She was lost and sensed that she was going the wrong way, but kept going. She ended up in the mountains at Big Bear Lake. When it started to get dark, she was anxious to get to her destination.

After checking her map, she found a freeway that would take her toward the ocean. She held her breath while the traffic rushed passed, leaving her standing still. She gripped her steering wheel for dear life. She was relieved when she saw her turn-off. Thank God for getting her off the freeways alive!

She was able to relax when she was on a familiar highway. She thought to herself, what was that all about? She could not help but smile when she thought about how much she loved the mountains. God wanted to show her that California has beautiful mountains too.

She stopped at her daughter Susan's house, when she arrived in Oxnard. She had hidden a key so that her mother could get in while she was at work. She was happy to see her daughter, who she knew was having some very serious personal and emotional problems. Her heart went out to her and she wanted to do all that she could to help. They talked and she tried to comfort her.

The next day she emptied her car at a friend's house. She made several phone calls to realtor friends, to let him know that she was looking for a home to buy.

She was concerned about the housing market. She was especially interested in a retirement community. She had heard that property values were on the rise and that it was a sellers market. She was afraid that she would be priced out of the market and unable to buy in a good area.

Three days after she had arrived, she was shown a couple of properties. One unit was vacant and in the area that she wanted. She put in an offer for quite a bit less and agreed to accept the unit "as is." The deal was accepted with a thirty thirty-day escrow. She had been approved in advance for financing and was able to close the deal within three weeks.

The community was forty years old with 773 units for seniors over fifty-five years old. A bonus room was attached to the garage and separated from her living area by a patio.

It was a relief having the keys to her front door again. The condominium was about two miles from her children and the same distance to the Pacific Ocean. She planned to rent out the back room to help with expenses.

It appeared as if God had been saving the home just for her! She had faith that God would guide and protect her. She was prepared to do whatever she needed to do in relocating. She was guarded against unrealistic expectations. When God says "yes," hang on and be prepared for doors to open.

*****

She had to be honest with herself in regards to her relationships with her children. She had been unavailable for years because of her drinking and commitment to sobriety. She was absent from their lives for another ten years when she lived in Colorado.

Now that she was living close, it would not be right for her to think that she could just walk back into their lives. She was going to have to earn their love and trust back.

She had to set aside all of her differences with her children's father if they were going to be a family. She had to give her ex-husband, the father of her children and grandfather, credit for all the years that he has helped their children and grandchildren. It would be extremely selfish of her to impose upon the relationship that he has established with them over the years.

She made a decision to accept the father of her children regardless of what she had to do or how long it would take. He was the last person on her list that she really needed to forgive. She had to put this relationship into a healthy perspective and love the unlovable, if she wanted to be free and at peace.

When she divorced Ben, it was a shock to the children. They never fought or argued in front of them. She had learned to keep her mouth shut most of the time when she was married. She stuffed fifteen years of hurt, anger and hatred that she had for the man. She kept her distance from him and avoided family gatherings if she knew that he would be there.

She wanted to be a part of the family and not apart from them. She would need to change her attitude and let go. She had prayed until her knees ached, wanting help with the bitterness and hatred. All the prayer in the world did not helped until she took the action to face the enemy and embrace her problem head on.

The first time that she showed up at a family gathering where their children's father was, the room went quiet. The grandkid's eyes got big; the oldest granddaughter could not help but find it funny. Barbara was uncomfortable, but determined to keep showing up and to avoid giving into negative emotions.

After a year of sharing holidays and birthdays, she was able to feel comfortable at family events. She had not thought about how their differences were affecting the children and grandchildren. The tension within the family began to go away. It was a relief not to be torn apart over family loyalties.

Over the last five years, she celebrated many family events with the children's father. They have been guests in each other's homes. When she looks at the man, she feels empathy. She was emotionally detached from what once separated them. She thanks God for giving time...time and healing.

As the result of her congenial reconciliation in the family, the void that once existed inside her for so many years was gone; this was an answer to her prayer.

She stepped aside and waited for opportunities to be helpful, any effort on her part had to be unconditional. Her children were not interested in what she had to say. She had to take an interest in what they were saying and doing.

Her children were planting their own gardens and pulling the weeds.

She never thought that she would live long enough to have grandchildren. She is blessed with seven grandsons and three granddaughters. She cannot describe in words how proud she is of her grandchildren and what great young adults they are becoming.

Becky's children, Brooke and Jeremy taught her how to be a grandmother. It was through them that the child in her was able to come out and play. They were fortunate to have shared many quality hours together in Colorado. She shares secrets and most importantly lots of love with them.

She has had many beautiful memories about her experiences with her grandchildren; she looks forward to many more years of sharing.

*****

God's Kid went on a mission back to Colorado Springs for a month to help her daughter Becky.

It had been four years since she had seen her AA friends at "Walk the Talk." They moved into a larger meeting room because their attendance has doubled. The group continues to share their love.

She could not help but smile when she saw the familiar faces in the group. She finds it hard to accept their compliments. She knows that the people are grateful and she does not want to invalidate their sincerity. She is especially pleased to see that God is still alive and well within the group.

On March 7, 2004, she will celebrate twenty-three years of continuous sobriety. It has been a long journey with many lessons and surrenders. Life has disciplined her and faith has saved her, it is by grace that she lives today. There is nothing haunting her from the past. She is an open book.

She is content with her relationship with God, others and herself. She believes that any wrongs that she may have done in the past imagined or real, have been long forgotten or forgiven. Her fears have been faced and erased.

The peace that surpasses all understanding lives in her soul and is unshakable as long as she keeps walking the walk.

It has been almost five years since she retired to Southern California. It took her a year to adjust and feel comfortable again. She was once told that financial insecurity may not leave but the fear will go away...

If she did not take action or change, she would have been spiritually paralyzed. When she gets ahead of God, fear of the unknown can take over. Only in retrospect can she see that God is still on the job. When this realization hits her, she cannot help but be astonished.

She thanks God for the ability to see when her thoughts are real or not. She can smile when her mind plays tricks on her.

She has been able to get excellent medical help in California that she could not have gotten in Colorado. She has found the most wonderful doctor who has taken a personal interest in her medical problems.

She has been making her little condominium a castle. She thanks God for the quality of life that she is able to enjoy in her later years. Had she waited a few more months, she would not have been able to afford to live in California. Property values in her area have more than doubled in the last five years.

She needed to fit into her new neighborhood so she volunteered for a couple committees. The senior residents are great teachers. So much of the senior's pasts have been forgotten and too soon, they will be forgotten.

*****

She gathered up all of her photo albums and pictures that she had kept in half a dozen different places. She sorted what she wanted to keep and what she wanted to dispose of. She put together a photo scrapbook of her mother and father's family and her first sixteen years.

In the process she contacted her brother, sister, and cousins for pictures. The elders were able to send her some very old pictures that she had copied and returned. There were pictures of relatives that she had not seen or known. She felt like she was on a treasure hunt and got excited each time she found another lost relative.

Wanda her sister, mentioned that they should have a family reunion in Michigan; she jumped at the idea. She spoke to some of her relatives and thought that it would be great if they could get together. Her nephew offered his home in the country for the get together.

Most of the relatives had longed for a family connection. The old feuds that once caused separation within the family have gone to the grave. There are no skeletons in the closet.

They had a date and place well in advance for the round up. God's Kid collected relative's addresses and spread the news about a round up. They contacted relatives who lived out of state so they would have plenty of time to make vacation arrangements.

When her nephew sent out notices to the addresses that she provided, he was in shock with the overwhelming response that he received. She could not help but laugh when her nephew stated that he did not know that he had that many relatives. There are no coincidences in God's world.

God's Kid went to Michigan where they had a fantastic catered round up. Her nephew's beautiful country home was an ideal place to gather. Family flew in from all over the U.S. A relative who was a professional photographer took some great pictures of this historical event.

*****

Family issues have been the hardest for her to resolve spiritually. She could not get it right without the help from her Higher Power.

Her being away from her immediate family in Colorado for ten years was the best thing that she could have ever done. With the miracle of time, her old wounds have healed.

There are no people, places or things that she finds unacceptable today. She has choices in her life and can side step the booby traps. She has let go of her expectations and can accept everyone and everything in God's world being exactly as it is suppose to be and not according to her perfectionist ideal.

We all walk the walk down different paths in life; the similarity is how we walk and where we choose to go. The result is the same, providing we maintain our spiritual condition and hold onto God's hand.

Her children and grandchildren will never do it her way; she has given them the right to be wrong and the right to be right. She once told her children that if she taught them to do something her way, it was probably wrong.

Relationships of any kind have provided her with an excellent opportunity to check in with herself and look at her defects.

*****

Her retirement has been one long vacation in many ways. She has been able to take a vacation from her vacation. It is wonderful to have days when there is nothing to do. She loves the sunny days when she can sit on her patio and watch the humming birds.

She remembers the days when she would cry herself to sleep from exhaustion. She asked God to let her live long enough so that she would know how it feels to do nothing. She never thought that day would arrive. Each and every day that she wakes up and is still breathing is a special gift. She does not take advantage the days when she can open her eyes and see the beauty around her.

God comes through, sometimes quickly and sometimes slowly.

She made reservations to spend a few days at Catalina Island with a friend. She was not feeling very good the morning that they were scheduled to leave. Her friend called and asked if she had seen the news. It was September 11, the day that we lost the Twin Towers in New York. After watching the unbelievable news, they debated whether they should go or not. She called and learned that the boats were still running to the island. They decided to go with reluctance and sadness.

The first night she was there, she started to run a very high temperature. They hurried home the next morning. She was in horrid pain by the time she got home. Her friend took her to the hospital where they did a MRI and was unable to find a cause for the pain. After a couple tests, the doctor had her sign a paper giving her consent for him to do what he had to do. .

She was very sick and had never experienced so much pain. When she signed the consent form, she thought that this might be it! She asked herself, if she was ready to go or not? She flashed back on her life and was at peace. As she had suspected, her appendix had burst.

When the day comes for her to take harp lessons, it will be the ultimate spiritual experience.

*****

BARBARA JEAN

"WHAT IF TOMORROW STARTS WITHOUT ME?"

When tomorrow starts without me and I am not there to see
If the sun should rise and find you with your eyes, filled with tears?
I wish so much you would not cry the way you did today
While thinking of the many things we did not get to say
I know how much you love me, as much as I love you
Each time that you think of me, I know you will miss me too
However, when tomorrow starts without me, please try to understand
That an angel came, called my name, and took me by the hand
And said my place was ready in heaven far above
That I would have to leave behind all those that I dearly love
However, when I walked through Heaven's gate I felt so much at home
When God looks down and smiled at me from his golden throne,
He said this is eternity and all I promised you
Today life on earth is past; a tear fell from my eye
For all my life, I had always thought I did not want to die
I had so much to live for, so much left to do
It seemed almost impossible that I was leaving you
I thought of all the yesterdays, the good ones and the bad
I thought of all the love we shared and all the fun we had
If I could relive yesterday, just for a while
I would say good-bye, kiss you, and maybe see you smile
Then I fully realized that this could never be
For emptiness and memories would take the place of me
And when I thought of worldly things, I might miss tomorrow
I thought of you and when I did, my heart was filled with sorrow
I was promised no tomorrows, for today will always last
And since each day is the same, there is no longing for the past
You have been so faithful, so trusting and so true
Though there were times, you did some things you knew you should not do
You have been forgiven and now at last you are free

Therefore, won't you come, take my hand, and share my life with me?
So when tomorrow starts without me, don't think we're far apart
For every time you think of me, I am right here in your heart.
Author Unknown

CHAPTER II

Remembering

"If we can see the patterns of our days, we could discern how devious
were the ways
that brought us to the present time...We should forget the hurts,
and the fears. To know that we could come no other way
or grow into our good
without the steps that our feet found so hard to take."
By Martha Smock

It is by the grace of God that she is able to see clearly how situations, people and places influenced her life today. She has been given the gifts of love, wisdom and understanding. Time has been a great healer and she has been able to detach from the lonely, scared, abused fearful child. She is convinced that she has experienced in life has made her the person that she is today.

She cannot completely close the door to her past. AA has been raising her for over twenty-three years and has given her the tools that have contributed to her recovery and way of life.

It is with clear eyes that she can see a helpless, innocent child, who was born at a time of war and uncertainty. She can imagine the hardship that her unmarried parents were having with another mouth to feed. Surviving the great depression and being in their forties, life must have been pure hell. They had nothing to give to themselves, let alone to small children.

There were no books around to teach parenting skills.

Her older brother was forced into taking care of her. She had a mother who could not mother and a brother who could not be a brother. They were children being raised by children.

They could not have known the effects that this would have on her. Perhaps she was more aware and sensitive because she was a girl. The very first emotions that she remembers were based on fear and hate.

She believes that her mother loved her, in her way. She was never told or shown love. She had no way of knowing the difference between love and hate. Being unable to identify what was missing or needed left the child very empty and lonely. Imagine the void! Her heart goes out to the child who ached for love and attention.

Her only salvation was to escape reality and to create her own world, imagined or real. She remembers the days when she laid on the grass gazing at the clouds in search of images, looking at the clouds in search of images, searching for something that she could identify with. She found comfort in solitude and isolation.

The man that she called Father was emotionally detached. He found relief in the beer joints and with other women. She remembers following him around, wanting to be picked up, hugged or given a gentle touch. She watched and waited for his acknowledgement that never came.

Her mother was exhausted and suffering from chronic depression. It took everything that she had to stay alive. She remembers seeing what she knows to be sadness in her mother's eyes. There was no laughter or joy in their house. She can understand now why her mother wanted to commit suicide.

Her older brother Bob was unwanted and unloved. He was severely disciplined as a young boy. By today's standards, it would be considered child abuse. He rebelled by striking out at her and being defiant toward anyone who got in his way.

She looked at some pictures taken in the forty's and saw that their family was not unique in what she considered poverty. Very few children had store-bought clothes then, the difference was that they appeared to have had better care. She always felt ugly compared to the other girls.

The very first act of kindness that she remembers came to her from a schoolteacher. This was so unfamiliar; she pulled away when she was shown affection.

Her older sister's visits were special because she would always bring them gifts. She knew that anything she cherished would be destroyed. It was not meant for her to own or have anything.

As an adult, she went to Michigan and met the child. She walked to the railroad tracks and watched a freight train pass. She knew that it was not going to suck her under; freight trains have a journey too. She looked inside the broken down barn and visualized the sad child sitting alone sucking her thumb. She grieved for the lonely child.

She noticed how the trees had grown and thought that like ourselves, if we do not grow, we die. She saw the large rock that was planted deep in the ground. All attempts to remove it had failed; the rock would not budge, solidly embedded in the ground, never to be removed. She thought about her foundation for living that was as solid as that rock.

The road in front of the old farmhouse is a dead end now. An expressway runs across what was the old country road. It is at the end of this road that she found a new beginning for the child.

This beautiful little girl with the snarls in her hair and wearing dresses made out of feed sacks, got affirmation that she is loved.

Her grand daughter Brooke taught the child in her to play. When she bought her special dolls and toys, she really bought them for her inner child. The lost child's spirit came alive with the help of a five-year-old grandchild.

When she returned to the small village that she was raised in, she had mixed feelings. The population is around 2,000; with many new beautiful homes built in the countryside. When she drove around the area, she had to search for familiar places.

She went to the store and looked for people who she had once known; she sensed that there were eyes staring at her. It had been many years since she had walked down the streets of her town. It was quite an experience visiting old memories. The churches and bars had not changed. She did not find any ghost; the angry, hopeless girl was nowhere to be found. All judgment that she had, was gone. They did not change, she changed, thank God.

She could not blame anyone for how she once felt and re-acted. What she saw was the simplistic beauty in everything and everyone. When she spoke to some of the village people, she realized how sacred their values were. She admired their faith and strength, especially within the families. She felt ashamed for all the years that she denied and despised the "hick town."

She drove up and down old Grand River between Lansing and Detroit. There was a time when she believed that this was the only road. She was an escapee of the community that inspired and motivated her to succeed, in spite of them. She owes an apology to the village and its people.

The one place that she did not visit was the school that she had been told to leave. She was in trouble on the first day she started school. She lacked concentration because of fear. The other students were very intimidating and overwhelming. In the fifty's they did not have the understanding and help that they have now. Kids with problems were discriminated against and picked on. It was black or white, either you are or you are not. You are a "have not" if you are poor. If you are labeled, you do not have a prayer.

It is impossible to achieve when there is separation. Each day at the desk was a struggle; it did not take much for the girl to give up. When she flunked the fifth grade, it confirmed the belief that she was stupid. She thought for years that she had a learning disability and was an academic failure. The girl fell through the cracks.

She is free and happy that her world has grown beyond the village and the school. She thanks God for the ability to be a success.

Many years later when her thirst to learn was stimulated, she had to prove to herself that she was not stupid. She sat in college classes with a smile on her face. She thought about the days when she was in school, as she moved forward.

When she was forced into getting a GED, it was ironic that she took the test in Michigan. She wanted to flash her achievements in the faces of the educators and scream, "See I am not dumb." Instead, she said a prayer for others like herself and for them not to give up, regardless of what adversity they run into.

There were times when she used her intellect to cover up her lack of formal education. She had a very deep resentment against her fifth grade teacher who failed her. She refused to open or own a book after the fifth grade.

She had not included the teacher on her resentment or amends list. Many years after being sober, it became clear that she needed to contact this teacher. She wrote her a letter and had her cousin deliver it to her since she did not have her address. She remembered the teacher as being very abrasive and aggressive.

She received a response back from the teacher that included

a book that she had written about the old one-room country schools. She read her book and took a special interest in the pictures of the kids that were included.

After she finished reading the book, she had a very different opinion of this teacher. She was able to understand how very committed and devoted she was toward her students. She felt relieved and free from the years of internal combat that she had with educators.

The adversity that she experienced was a primary driving force for her to achieve. She had to be strong so that she could prove her worth to the world. She had an inferiority complex that at times manifested it's self as a superiority complex. This played a major part in her success and covering up what was really going on in her personal life.

She remembers feeling ugly as a teenager. She did not have decent clothes for the cold Michigan winters. She had lost a front tooth and it was months before her mother could afford the thirty-five dollars for a partial plate. She had a deep inner sadness and no sense of belonging. Her eyes were dull and her face was expressionless as she kept her head down looking at the ground. With a lack of identity or self worth, she vented outwardly at anyone and everything.

She tried to get in touch with the teenager who was an outcast and searching for love in an insane environment. It was impossible for her to take care of herself when no one else gave a damn. She was labeled and judged for something that she did not understand.

She had no dreams or hope for the future. There was nothing and nobody that she could go to for help or advice. She existed and carried within herself nothing but emptiness. She ached for someone to love her.

When she thinks about her teen years, she knows that

she was not bad, she just felt bad. The places and people that she chose to be around were not evil; the labeling was nothing more than lies. Every action and reaction that she had was just a camouflage. Deep in her heart, there was no malice, just fear and hurt.

She thanks God for everything that she did or did not do in her teen years.

She was forced to attend the church for many years without missing a Sunday. When she was bad, her mother made her attend prayer meetings. She was told repeatedly how sinful she was.

She can look back and see where her perfect attendance became beneficial to her adult life and work ethics...

When she attended the Church with a crooked steeple, she paid back the money that she had stolen.

Many of the beautiful little Old Ladies were still sitting in the same seats that they had sat in for forty years. She tuned out the preacher's sermon and admired the interior of the old building. She saw the magnificence of the stained glass windows that created rainbows of light. She admired the beautiful wood carved accents and decorative plaster walls. Behind the podium, was the baptismal tub that she had seen her mother being baptized.

While the preacher was doing his job trying to save souls, she entertained herself by catching flies with her hands. She did not intend to be rude, maybe a little bit of rebel was coming out.

As a prodigal child, she admired the construction of the church building. She was able to view it as a home for God's kids, not the house of God. The old time religion is just that, old time religion. She thought that God sat in the church balcony checking his list to see who was naughty and who was nice. She used to think that God was all seeing and all knowing and that she could not hide from Him. There was no doubt in her mind that God was going to send her down to the fires of hell.

She had to respect what the church did for her mother; she found grace and sanity in this church. If it had not been for the church she would have been insane or dead, she found hope there.

Barbara got her fundamental belief of a God in this Church. She understands that her God is not religious. She is forever grateful to the little brick church.

She attended services with her mother whenever she was in Michigan. After church, they would go to the coffeehouse near the expressway. Her mother's friends would join them for brunch. She looked forward to Sunday's fellowship with her mother and the ladies of grace.

Barbara was free to see how the love of God manifests, regardless of where or how we worship. She can sit in any church, in any city, of any denomination and be comfortable.

She is glad that God does not have a face and that He is not someone who she can touch and see.

She has learned to love the old house on Church Street. Her mother lived there for over forty years and made it home. It was obvious that she found peace and comfort in her old age. Her special touches reflected the love that she had for her sanctuary. All her making nice and years of patient crocheting personalized the rooms.

After her mother passed away, the house was sold. She had to let go of her key that she had held onto for years. She visited the property since the new owners took over. Like everything else in her past, it had changed.

She was twelve years old when she started to look for work so she could have some money. The first few dollars she earned was spent on badly needed clothes. After that, she had to be responsible for all personal items that she needed. She had been so deprived that she was willing to do what she could to make money.

She would rake leaves, sell the Grit newspaper, shovel snow and baby-sit in the day. She got a lot of personal satisfaction and independence when she had a few dollars in her pocket. She knew that there were no free rides. It was up to her to work and make it happen.

When she was fourteen, she washed dishes at a truck stop from 4:00 to midnight. She would go to school to sleep. She also helped her mother at the laundry matt folding and ironing clothes for customers. In addition, she had to cook and clean for her family. Her mother believed that if she were kept busy, she would not have time or the energy to get into trouble.

When she was married, she was constantly reminded that she was a leach and a free-loader. With four small children, she worked part-time at a country school cleaning and watching the kids at recess and lunch hour.

After moving to California, she cleaned rental property to help subsidize their expenses. That same employer encouraged her to get a real estate license. She got the validation that she needed from real estate. She worked on and off in real estate for over twenty years. She was good with numbers and did accounting when the market was bad.

It did not matter how much money she made; it did not satisfy her emotional need for love and happiness. She made a lot less money then what she led people to believe. Almost every cent that she made was used for investments or her family's needs.

She wanted people to think that she was rich so they would give her respect and acceptance. It was all a game of "let's pretend." She was driven by the success, until situations changed and she realized that she hated and valued nothing. When she was drunk, she hated her home and everything in it. Nothing and nobody could make her happy.

She did not wait for God to bring apples to her door. She had been a risk taker with marriages, employers and life. When her expectations failed, she would get out of control and be self-destructive.

In spite of the failures and rejection, she did not give up completely. When times were the hardest she would exercise her spiritual muscle and regroup. She was forced to learn from every mistake or experience and to become aware of how self-centered she was. If she did not take the lessons seriously, she was doomed to repeat them. She had to get honest with herself and change what she could. She did not want to waste the growing pains; her only failure was when she stopped trying.

Every position that she has ever had in the work force has helped her to become a better employee. She never left a job without taking valuable experiences down the road. Once the emotional fog left her, she was able to see clearly what she did or did not do. It became a stepping-stone to something better, when doors closed windows opened.

She never thought that the job she would come to love would be with a major corporation. Sitting in a tiny cubical that she shared, plugged into a headset staring at a computer and being abused by customers, was definitely not what she had wanted her last job to be like.

When she had bad days, she found comfort in a small poster that she kept in her cubical that said, "I love this place, I am too old for a paper route, too young for social security and too tired to have an affair." That said it all for her.

On another wall in her cubical, she had the Prayer of Saint

Francis. The humor and prayers got her through many tough days.

Coming from dysfunctional backgrounds, her husband did not know how to be a husband., she did not know how to be a wife. Being such opposites in so many ways, it is amazing that they stayed married for fifteen years.

He rebelled against her by not communicating and sexually and emotionally abusing her.

It is a miracle that she survived her marriage with any sanity. They lived in two very different worlds and came from two very different backgrounds. The only common interest that they had was their commitment to their four children. She questions the sincerity of his affection for his children. The man was dead emotionally and incapable of feeling.

If anyone tells you opposites attract, do not believe them. She lived on false hope for years. She believed that if she did certain things, it would get better between them. She lied to herself a thousand times because she wanted the marriage to work. The marriage was an endurance contest from the beginning; both of them existed in pure misery.

She wanted to make love happen between them. She did believe that their children and finances was the only reason that she hung on for so long.

He told her the night that they married, how he was going to make her pay for trapping him. The marriage was a struggle with his need to control and dominate. His many selfish and unreal demands made her his slave and not a wife. The more oppressed and beaten down she was, the more he would impose his power over her.

He played sick games and set traps and when she fell into his snare, he would verbally tear her apart. She was emotionally stalked. She lived in constant fear of this man. When things were going smooth between them, she knew it was not going to last. He was taking notes and looking for excuses to attack.

She was compared to a horse that needed to have its spirit broken. She was without solutions to the physical, mental, emotional and sexual abuse. He never once said that he was sorry or showed any remorse for what he had done.

She saw the pleasure that he got from his assaults. For a long time she accepted the punishment and thought it was because she was a rotten wife and mother. She was not able to confide in anyone about her situation. She had one friend who she shared babysitting with. When she told her about the marriage, the friend said, "It couldn't be true, he was such a nice person." She saw his extreme moods and personality changes when he was around other people.

In 1950's the phrase, "domestic abuse" was unknown or taboo. You did not air your dirty laundry in public. It was kept behind closed doors. It was something that was not talked about. It was the husband's duty to bring home the paycheck and the wife was an employee. The closets in many homes were full of family skeletons and abuse was quickly covered up.

She was a hostage in her marriage. It was also said that, "you made your bed and now you have to lay in it."

She was a broken woman who wanted to die many times over. The love that she had for her children was her salvation. She had no identity or self-worth.

No human being should ever have to endure that hell. She understands why battered women stay in abusive relationships. How easy it is to be trapped and tricked. She can see how intimidation, invalidation, being deprived, controlled and denied can make one an easy target for abuse.

She was able to see the patterns in her life, of how and why her relationships with men had been damaging. The healthier that she became, the more aware she was of how ignorant and naive she had been. The more that she discovered, the better she could recover.

For over two years, she was on fire with anger over her discoveries. The cause and effect became very clear. It would be impossible for her to have any peace until she could let go of her experiences. For over forty years, she harbored hatred and was eaten alive with silent rage. She prayed and prayed for God to take away her pain. There were days when she was so desperate for help that she laid on the floor face down, begging God to help.

She had so much contempt that she could not stand to be in the same room as the man. She had to fight to keep from verbally exploding and visualizing him dead. She had to separate herself from the family celebrations. She had to stop pretending and selling herself out for the sake of family.

Her children are the love of her life. She would trade her life for anyone of her children. They gave her a reason for living and strength. In spite of her lack in mothering skills, she did the best that she could, considering what she had or did not have.

She was not a very affectionate mother nor was she patient. She took care of her children's personal needs and was rarely away from them. She was not able to be there for them emotionally. She gave all the love that she had the only way she knew how. She sacrificed herself and pretended that all was well so there could be peace in the home. Her children validated her existence.

She made her home comfortable for her family. Home is and probably always will be very special to her. She would over compensate with what she did not have. She worked very hard for security and success. She got the validation that she needed as a professional woman who thrived on her accomplishments.

There were many lost years, or were they really lost?

The pain was so deeply embedded into the woman's soul, she prays. "The man is sick; forgive him for he does not know what he is doing." She knows that she has to let go if she is going to heal.

She thanks God for not giving her anymore than what she can understand and accept. It has taken her years of honesty and soul-searching to see the why's and how's. In the process, she has developed a wonderful, open understanding of situations and why she reacted the way she did.

It is clear to her that the effects from her childhood and young adult life had taken aggressive control of her actions for many years; it goes way beyond feelings and facts. When she lacks understanding, she becomes confused, frustrated and exhausted.

Her life was a circus with her in the middle hanging onto the trapeze, spinning.

With help, she was able to reach into the core of her soul and humbly embrace every event and person who was on her path. The deeper she dug, the more amazed she became with each new insight. She is able to set aside most of her past and be fully conscious of outside influences and patterns. With this knowledge, she is able to be the person who she has always wanted to be. She is confident when she gives herself approval for all the right reasons.

She did not know who she was and when she began to find herself, she did not know what to do. Thank God, she can just be herself. She has been relieved from fear, remorse, grief and the anger that she carried around most of her life. She does not have to hide, pretend or prove anything to anyone, especially to herself.

It was necessary for her to explore every corner and path

of her life. It was equally important for her to retrace her walk physically and to discover what she was or was not. This involved a lot of self-obsessing. She dug deep into the mind and spirit of a neglected, abused child, a rebellious teen-ager, battered wife, a mother, career woman and an alcoholic.

There were times that she had intense internal gut-wrenching pain; when she explored, there was also overwhelming relief and joy.

Without faith in God, she could not have taken the first step. She would fall to her knees with each new revelation and wanted to scream at the top of her lungs to the heavens, "hallelujah!" When she realized how much emotional power she had given to people and situations, she was amazed...

Over time when she separated the old self from the new self, she gradually experienced a death-taking place. The death of old ideas and her way of behaving and thinking were dying.

She felt blessed and considered all the miracles in her life to be sacred.

She began to understand, the why and how her character defects developed. She saw how the attitude of indifference came from the neglect and abuse. It was a learned behavior to click into another channel and ignore what or who was around her. She kept this persona in all her affairs. She was good at faking and pretending when reality was too much for her to accept. She did not allow her heart to open because of her fear that it would be broken. She did not have any ideas or examples of kindness or love in her world. Her views of life were ugly and bleak. It took everything that she had to keep breathing in and out.

There was so much loneliness that her insides felt hollow and empty. The lack of communication other than being yelled at echoed in her ears. The complete lack of affection damaged her ability to have intimacy in future relationships. It is impossible to love when you have never been loved. The heart goes cold and freezes.

Children definitely become what they are taught and unless she wanted to spend the rest of her life in an emotional jail, she had to unlearn and relearn.

Before she could experience love, she had to learn to love herself. Having gone through life with no self-esteem or identity this appeared to be an impossible challenge. She knew what the problem was and how or where it came from…She just did not know what it was going to take to undo the damage.

She learned about love from "The Course in Miracles." The book gave her the answers she had questioned all of her life. It was in the "Course" that she learned the truth about God…

As she read the book, she absorbed every single word and processed the message with a thirst. The truth became her new reality and hope. She forced herself to reach out and in the reaching; she began to feel twinges in her heart.

When she got all the ghosts out of her closet, she was a surprised to learn that they were illusions. She stared evil in the face and saw her twisted concept of reality. She realized that the church was not her enemy and that her personal experiences were polluting her translation.

She internalized and personalized every experience that she had encountered. She was a student of life with some very poor teachers. She was without a means to sort the good from the bad; she took it all in and ran on empty.

She demanded to have the hole in her gut filled. Unknowingly she sought help in many ways from many people. She had volunteered to be a victim; thriving on responsibility until she collapsed in bed from exhaustion. There was no balance; it was all or none. She escaped by trying to be superwoman.

She needed to be needed and got outside validation from

her personal achievements. When she realized, that she was not super-woman or God's caretaker, she was able to quit pushing herself. She discovered that her unsatisfied need for appreciation and acknowledgement was her driving force.

She had to make some major changes and learn to practice sloth. It took her over two years to talk, think, drive, and eat more slowly. She became aware of how compulsive she was. She would act first and work things out later. Usually she would be up to her rear in alligators before she opened her eyes.

The most beautiful gift that she received was the discipline and discovery that she was not deprived and the empty holes in her gut were gone.

She tried retail therapy to satisfy her wants. All she got was huge credit card bills. She has two lists, one of her wants and another of her needs. The wants list was very long and her needs list was very short. Over time, she has been able to satisfy some of her wants and her needs have always been taken care of.

She could not imagine herself being happy. She could not remember a day in her life that she was truly happy. She looked toward others to make her happy, but like her, they were seeking the same. There is a very slight chance of success when two un-happy people are depending on something that will only elude them.

She had to develop trust in herself before she could trust others. She depended upon her spiritual advisor's help when she had to making major decisions. To this very day, when she is in doubt, she will ask a special closed-mouth friend for advice.

She has not stopped being teachable and there is so much to relearn. All of her experiences have taught her the wisdom to know the difference. When the yellow lights flash, she backs away and waits. She allows herself to get just so close and when flags go up, she pays attention. It is easy for her to get into situations that baffle her. Getting out can be very hard.

Her self-centered nature always wants to be satisfied regardless of who or what comes her way. Knowing this, she is constantly on guard and honest about her motives. It is impossible to be 100% free from self-centeredness. When in doubt she calls upon God for spiritual guidance.

She is not a magnet to insanity or abuse. She has given up on trying to fix or change the world. She can stand still when she is powerless over people, places and things. She is not trying to take control unless it becomes a threat to her self-preservation. She can accept the thing that she cannot change, that does not mean she has to like it. She can only change herself.

*****

Original Serenity Prayer

God, grant me the serenity to accept the things that I cannot change.
The courage to change the things that I can and the wisdom to know the difference.
Living one day at a time, accepting hardship as a pathway to peace,
Taking as Jesus did this sinful world as it is, not as I would have it.
Trusting that you will make things right if I surrender to your will
So that I may be reasonably happy in this life and supremely happy
With you forever in the next.
Written by Reinhold Niebuhr

*****

She does not take everyone that she meets home to her family. She can sincerely say that she has not met anyone in a long time that she does not like. She may avoid toxic personalities or cringe at something that she saw. As long as no one deliberately steps on her toes, it is none of her business. Thank God, she is not the judge and jury of the world. What a relief!

She has made some wonderful friends along the way that she will cherish for life. It is through friendships that she has learned how to be a friend. She does not make plans for their lives and futures; she rides piggyback.

When she meets an old friend there is no time gap, regardless of how long it had been since their last visit. They do not take advantage of each other, but enhance one another's lives. They remain loyal and respectful and know that they are blessed. Each day, event or occasion that we are able to be friends is cherished. It does not matter if they are male or female, the quality of friendship remains the same.

It is a great freedom not having to be God's caretaker. We cannot always give what we do not have. She can remain silent, smile and give a hug while she says a silent prayer.

She has many mirrors in her home. For years, she avoided looking at her reflection. Now when she passes by a mirror she can see a beautiful person. When she goes to sleep, she is not haunted with horrible nightmares. She has dreams that are beautiful and peaceful.

She can open her heart and sincerely love her children and grandchildren. She is still experimenting and learning to be unconditional without expectations. Instead of thinking about what she wants or needs from them, she looks for what she can add to their lives. She does not want them to try to understand her; that would just make them goofy. It is easier for her to give understanding.

It would be completely unrealistic and impossible for anyone to identify or relate to her life unless they have walked in her slippers.

There was a time that she could identify with the song, "I

Am a Rock." She was dead emotionally and had no tears in her cup. She was unable to laugh or cry for many years. She remembers the first time that she really laughed it startled her.

She remembers the first time that she cried in many years. She was listening to someone share at an AA meeting that made her very sad. The tears did not come from negative emotions, hurt or pain but from sincere empathy that she felt for another suffering human being. Her world and life had been a very small, dark place. She walked the walk and experienced a living hell. She was paralyzed by fear and restored by faith. She was given freedom beyond anything she could ever imagine. She has known the overwhelming tears of joy and the peace that surpasses all understanding. She has known love that goes beyond words. She has been able to maintain her balance and focus.

She has created her own sanctuary for her soul and can retreat in solitude knowing that she is not alone. She can give herself a hug and knows that from the hair on the top of her head to the bottom of her feet, she is all right. She loves beauty, simplicity, and being surrounded with beautiful memories. As long as she keeps the faith, she can have balance, order, cleanliness and warmth in her home. It reflects the peace and comfort that she feels.

She is grateful that she is at a time and place in her life where she can soak in the happiness. She is able to delight in the sights, sounds and smells that surround her. She is able to take her little dog to the ocean and go for walks with God. Her blue eyes have grown large and very little passes her sight that she does not take delight in. When she closes her eyes at night, she can reflect on the day and thank God.

She goes out of her way at times to find beauty. She delights at the sounds of the birds when they raise their voices in the morning to welcome another day. She loves the sound of the ocean surf and seeing Jonathan's seagulls. She loves music that caresses her soul and the smell of the flowers. There are days when she sits in the sun and watches the flowers grow with the eyes of a child.

The more harmony and balance that she has in her life, the more love and happiness she can experience, it is hard to have one without the other.

She thanks God for the writers who have shared their gift of words. Books have opened her mind and have helped to heal her heart. Her dreams have become reality in ways that is a mystery to her. Her illusions have exploded with a new form of reality that is beautiful. She has an opportunity to take out the trash.

She sometimes thinks that Moses and she were buddies. They had walked together for forty years in the desert, searching.

There is a little sadness remaining for the neglected child, rebellious teen and battered wife. Thank God, she is okay and enjoying the adventure. It is frightening to think that she could have given up after the first miracle.

While she remained faithful to others, she was being a hypocrite. She remained silent for peace at any price. She suppressed all the rage in the deep corners of her soul that ate at her like a cancer. She was afraid of herself when the anger surfaced; she tried to pray away the hatred. The harder and longer that she prayed, the deeper it was buried. She prayed hard and wanted forty years of abuse to go away. She had to stay away from her family and friends for a couple of years because she did not want to transfer her anger toward them.

When she exploded with rage, she would beat on her car steering wheel or anything else that was near, until the palms of her hands were black and blue. For her survival, it was necessary for the anger to run its own course. If her character is maliciously attacked, fire can come out of her ears. She will defend her values and beliefs with a passion. She will take action if anyone, including her family, attempts to be abusive toward her. She believes that God does not want to have his kids being abused or suffering.

Fortunately, she has not had to defend herself in a long time against any form of abuse. Her self-esteem and self-worth is too precious to walk on.

Slowly and she means slowly, God helped her to heal with each step she took. She realized how starved she was spiritually. She thanks God that she was exposed to the Good Book and a church. Maybe she was really saved in that church after all and just did not know it.

She mentioned to her son that, "someone must have been praying for her." He told her "he had been praying for her."

She was sensitive about having been called a fanatic and sold out. Today she would not hesitate to yell from the top of the tallest mountain her commitment to God and her passion for life. Her feet are planted in concrete and her faith is edged in granite.

While living in Colorado, one of the girls that she was helping wanted to go to the mountains for a 3rd-step. This is such a major spiritual commitment. She always asked whomever she was helping to choose a place that they wanted to go to for this step. It was a beautiful day as they drove into the Rocky Mountains. She was guided to a magnificent view near a canyon surrounding the mountains. They got on their knees.

She told the girl to say the prayer aloud with her. The girl screamed at the top of her lungs almost shaking the mountains. This was one of the beautiful moments that she has shared.

The healthier that she became, the more she could see when

she reflected or compared. Her old self has met the new self and intuitively she has learned how to handle situations that used to be baffling. She was given the freedom to let go of the past guilt, blame, shame and pain so the rooms of her heart could heal.

Self-honesty is a very long process of self-examination that has taken her years. Thank God for not giving her more than she could handle. One day at a time, more is revealed! Piece by piece and bit by bit, more is revealed.

She had hoped that someday she would be a free woman. Little did she realize that any freedom that she had hoped for would be lost in a bottle of whiskey? It took what it took, every single drop of liquor.

*****

The Program

She found a program designed and administered by a bunch of ex-drunk's whose only qualification for membership is that they cannot hold their liquor and have stopped trying to learn how.

The program has no rules, no dues and no fees, no nothing that any sensible organization seems to require.

At meetings they speak of one subject and wind up talking about something completely different and conclude by saying that we don't know anything about the program except that it works.

The groups are always broke, yet they have money to pay for rent and keep the coffeepot full. They are always losing members, but they seem to keep growing. They claim it is a selfish program but they always seem to be doing something for others.

Each group passes laws, rules, edits and pronouncements, which everyone blithely ignores. Members who disagree with anything are privileged to walk out in a huff, quitting forever, only to return as though nothing happened and are greeted accordingly.

Nothing is planned more than twenty-four hours ahead, yet great projects are born and survive magnificently. Nothing is according to Hoyle, so how can it survive?

Perhaps it is because we have learned to live and laugh at ourselves. God made man/woman and God made laughter, too. Perhaps, God is pleased with our disorganization efforts and makes things run right no matter who is pushing the wrong buttons. Maybe God is pleased because we are trying to be nobody but ourselves.

Author Unknown

CHAPTER 12

Walking the Walk

She makes a point of inviting God to dinner with her. When she says grace, the food tastes better.

She loves the smell of perfume on her clean bed sheets. She enjoys listening to music and appreciates those who have the gift of song. She loves it when there is nothing but stillness and quiet, knowing that she is at peace. It makes her happy when the phone rings with a friendly voice calling to ask how she is.

In some ways, she thinks that she has been chosen for a spiritual way of life. She does not want to relive her past life experiences nor does she want anyone to suffer as she did. She is grateful that she has lived long enough to have two lives. God understands when she takes time to check in, even when she is having a challenging day.

She plays games with God as her way of expressing her appreciation and thanks for what she has been given. The objective of her game is not to be found out when she helps or gives. If she is caught in the act of helping, it does not count. She believes it is not what she takes from this world but what she gives back.

She has been known to give too much and it has caused others to be uncomfortable. She has to learn to be sensitive toward others so they will not feel obligated. God is working with her on this so she does not alienate or impose on her friends values.

She did not understand what it meant when she heard that

the road gets narrow. While walking the walk, she has run into dead ends, block walls and forks in the road. She has had to turn around, hit her knees and make wiser choices on the highways of life. When she gets on the wrong path, it is usually because her motives were not aligned with God's will.

She would ask, what is God will for her? The answer is simple, to love, be happy, joyous and free. The 12-steps took her out of bondage. When she takes it back, she is in bondage. This goes against the spiritual principals and can cause conflict with relationships.

The good news is that when we love unconditionally and let go of our expectations we can be free. If we love God, life and sobriety as much as we love each other, it is possible for us to have spiritual relationships.

She has seen some of God's kids getting lost on the road to recovery. Some have had accidents caused by self-will or just forgot. Others have been rescued from the weeds. The journey can be long and hard. The ones, who walk into the doors of recovery and stay, are given many blessings. Some have given up before they would allow their Higher Power to take their hands.

When it comes to spiritual matters, stay with us so that we can love you until you can love yourself.

*****

The 12-Steps

Step 1   She learned about acceptance
Step 2   She learned about faith
Step 3   She learned about surrender and trust
Step 4   She learned about honesty
Step 5   She learned about courage
Step 6   She learned about willingness
Step 7   She learned about humility

Step 8   She learned about forgiveness
Step 9   She was given freedom
Step 10   She learned about perservence
Step 11   She learned about patience
Step 12   She learned about charity and love

FIRST STEP PRAYER

Today, I ask for help with my addiction. Denial has kept me from seeing how powerless I am and how my life is unmanageable. I need to learn and remember that I have an incurable illness and that abstinence is the only solution.

SECOND STEP PRAYER

I pray for an open mind so that I may come to and believe in a Power greater than I believe. I pray for humility and a continued opportunity to increase my faith. I do not want to be goofy anymore.

THIRD STEP PRAYER

God, I offer myself to Thee to build with me and to do with me as Thou wilt. Relieve me of the bondage of self that I may better do Thy will. Take away my difficulties, that victory over them may bear witness to those I would help, of Thy power, Thy love and Thy way of life, may I do Thy will always. (Big Book)

FORTH STEP PRAYER

Dear God, it is I who has made a mess of my life. I have done it and cannot undo it. My mistakes are mine and I will begin a searching and fearless moral inventory. I will write down all my wrongs to others. I will also include that which is good. I pray for strength to complete the task.

FIFTH STEP PRAYER

Dear God, my inventory has shown me who I am; yet I ask for your help in admitting my wrongs to another person and to You. Assure me and be with me *in this step that will begin my healing in recovery. With your help, I will see the cause and effect of my actions.*

SIXTH STEP PRAYER
Dear God, I am ready for your help in removing from me the defects of character, which I now realize, is an obstacle to my healing. Help me to continue to be honest with myself and guide me toward spiritual health.

SEVENTH STEP PRAYER
My Creator, I am now willing that you should have all of me, good and bad. I pray that you will remove from me every single defect of character, which stands in the way of my usefulness to You and others. Grant me strength as I go out from here to do your bidding. (Big Book)

EIGHTH STEP PRAYER
Dear God, I ask your help in making a list of all (including myself) that I have harmed (by thought, word, deed or action). I will take responsibility for my mistakes and be forgiving to others as You are forgiving to me. Grant me the willingness to begin my restitution.

NINTH STEP PRAYER
Dear God, I pray for the right attitude to make amends, being ever mindful not to harm others in the process. I ask for Your guidance in making direct and indirect amends. Most importantly, I will continue to make amends by staying abstinent, helping others and growing in spiritual progress.

TENTH STEP PRAYER
I pray that I might continue to grow in understanding and effectiveness. To take daily spot check inventories of myself, to correct mistakes when I make them. To take responsibility for my actions, to be aware of my negative and self-defeating attitudes and behaviors, to keep my willingness in check, to always remember that

I need Your help, to keep love and tolerance of others as my code and to continue in daily prayer how I can best serve You.

ELEVENTH STEP PRAYER

Dear God, as I do or do not understand, I pray to keep my connection with You open and clear from confusion of daily life, through my prayers and meditation, I ask especially for freedom from self-will, rationalizing, and wishful thinking. I pray for guidance of correct thought and positive action. Your will, not mine.

TWELFTH STEP PRAYER

Dear God, my spiritual awakening continues to unfold. The love that I have received, I shall pass on and give to others, both in and out of the fellowship. For this opportunity, I am grateful. I pray most humbly to continue walking the walk on the road of spiritual progress. I pray for the inner strength and wisdom to practice this way of life in all that I do and say.
Author Unknown

*****

She thanks God for the courage and the ten years that she lived in Colorado. At the time, she was open and willing to experience what is in front of her. Never in a thousand years, could she have known what a difference those years would have on her life.

When she left California, she was at an emotional bottom in relationships, health, employment and finances. She was empty and all her old ideas had stopped working. Her faith was the only thing that she had left; there were no other options.

She had to believe that God was embracing her tired soul when she took a giant leap of faith into the unknown. Over the years, she has been able to thank God when she has had to let go. It is impossible for her to be miserable if she keeps an attitude of gratitude. If she had not let go completely, she would not have the wisdom to know the difference.

No amount of money can buy the miracles and healing that she experienced in Colorado.

With every struggle and change, her faith got stronger. She did not give up or deny that a divine power was walking with her. There were many times when she asked God, "How much more do I have to go through?" She was spiritually dependent and did not give up believing that her experiences had value. God had not promised her that life was going to be easy. She was promised that God would always be near.

It is clear to her that every experience that she has ever had (good and bad) is her greatest assets. She appreciates today more because of the yesterdays. She prayed for discernment and had her prayer answered in ways that she could not have never have imagined.

Today she is free to walk the walk, with the knowledge that God is truly doing for her what she cannot do. She and God are getting older and take more time to sit and rest together. Her days are not manic and there is no urgency to do and be everything to everyone. She is not lost trying to get out of the maze, nor is God having a hard time keeping up with her. She walks with her head up and in grace. She does not have to be defensive and can trust others. If she becomes a victim, it is because she volunteered. She can look people in the eye and smile.

When she thinks of how blessed that she is, it makes her want to shout, thank-you. Nothing, absolutely nothing belongs to her. She came into this world with nothing and she will go out with nothing. What she has is on loan and what she does with it is her gift back to God. She loves her children and grandchildren, her friends, her home, nature, the beach, her dog and God.

When she lived in Colorado, she met people who cared and looked out for each other. The view of Pikes Peak is edged in her mind. She had a beautiful view from her front yard and from the windows at work. She saw God's majestic beauty in breathtaking mountains, sunsets and rainbows.

She could not have found a more wonderful place in the world for healing. She returned to Colorado Springs after being absent for four years. It is not that she did not want to visit earlier. First, she had to get her feet firmly planted in California. She wanted to be physically and mentally present. When she was back in Colorado, it was very hard for her to leave.

She believes that God does work through people. She has heard his message come through some of the most unlikely sources. She gave up questioning God and herself.

She has had the honor of meeting some fantastic people who, like herself, are just doing life on life's terms. They have touched each other in ways that transcends the love that one friend can have for another.

She remembers how suspicious she was when someone was being kind and questioned their motives. The people of the heartland are naturally friendly and trusting. If she needed help it was an insult not to ask. She can be very independent until she is forced to reach out. She was amazed at how anxious others were to help her. It is easier for her to give than to receive.

Her life has gone full circle with self-meeting self. She has repeated many of her old life experiences in her new life. The differences are that she is not walking alone and has choices. There have been hundreds of men and women, who have touched her life. Some in small ways and others in very profound ways; they have all given her a part of themselves. She did not always realize what they had said or done until later. She is amazed at how their influences have become her reality.

She has stolen their words, their examples, their love, their strength and their God. Her relationship with each one of them is sacred. We have all been teachers and students to each other. She is in touch with how very fragile we are and how short our lives can be. There are no guarantees, each day is a gift when we wake up and are still breathing.

She was once told that she was a woman with a steel rod down her spine, very rigid. She was offended by this comment until she realized that she was lacking flexibility because of her perfectionist ideals.

She did not want to mess up her recovery by doing something stupid. There is no perfect way of doing the program of recovery other than not drinking one day at a time. She tried to over compensate with the 12-steps and got discouraged. Perfectionism can also be another form of control.

Having worked for a major corporation that was experiencing growing pains, she learned that "Gumby" was their mascot. If she wanted to be a worker among workers, she had to be flexible. She was forced to surrender to authority and remain open to the company's many changes.

She once stated that she did not like the instructional environment, yet, she worked for a Corporation. Her prayer for patience was tested and answered.

When dealing with the public she became acutely aware of her character defects and personality flaws. She was once told to pray for sweetness. Besides patience and flexibility, she learned to be sweet even when she did not want to be. After a couple years of faking it, she realized that she had become sweeter.

God was listening to her prayers. She knows when to walk away with a prayer on her lips. She can no longer plea ignorance and accepts wisdom with a grateful heart. Today she takes smaller steps; she is getting too old to leap very far anymore.

She has watched her grandchildren and has noted how beautifully they are developing into responsible adults. She hopes that her love and example will help them to make good choices.

She was once told to watch children's behavior at a playground and identify with the similarities. At the time, she thought that this was really a stupid thing for her to do. Now she is glad that she watched the kids. Yes, there is a lot similarity.

She continues to pray for her four adult children as they walk their own walk without too many skinned knees.

Life can be a real disciplinarian force and regardless of how hard or long we fight, life will always win.

The disease that tells us that we do not have a disease is alive and well within her family.

She continues to think often of her many special friends, who have shown up in her life exactly when she needed them. She has been blessed by their presence when she did and did not want to be bothered. Pretty words cannot express her gratitude for the gifts that they have added to her life. She is proud to be your spiritual friend. The bonds such as theirs are for life, regardless of what roads we have chosen. We still have a lot of work to do and it is not over until it is over.

She has never believed more strongly, that we are exactly where we are supposed to be, doing exactly what we are supposed to be doing. We are right on God's schedule in this journey. There are no absolutes and none of us is going to get it completely right in this lifetime.

There is so much to unlearn and relearn that there are not enough years in an average lifetime to make all the corrections. She thinks God has a definite plan and purpose for each and everyone of us. At one time or another in our lives, we get a call.

Like her, many will wait until they are desperate before they hear the voice.

Others will die fighting because they are stuck in the mess and do not realize that they have choices.

She thanks God for faith and believing that things would get better. She discovered that, not only did it get better it got different.

She has not given up on her hopes and dreams; she just does not plan the results. She does not drink, use or abuse, "one day at a time." The days have added up and given her many wonderful years...

Her heartaches when she sees the faces whose eyes are blank. She delights when she sees their lights come back on; their miracles bring a smile to her face.

There was a time when she had survivor's remorse and guilt because she was given a second life. Over the years, she has observed those who have not gotten it or forgotten. She saw them spinning out of control with lying, denying, justifying and rationalizing. Living with illusions and ignoring the truth. Wishing and wanting things to change, but still doing the same old things repeatedly. Trapped by the insanity and fighting for freedom from pain and suffering, unwilling to surrender or change.

She did not know that there was a way for her to recover from a dysfunctional alcoholic life. She is not unique. By the grace of God and Alcoholics Anonymous, she found a new way of living. She thanks God for AA and thanks AA for her God.

When her time comes to go to the big meeting in heaven, she wants to have a smile on her face and peace in her soul, knowing that she did not waste the time that she was given.

She likes to compare her recover process to that of an artichoke. Over the days, months and years, she has pealed away one leaf at a time. When all the leaves have been removed, she finds the tender heart of the artichoke.

She remembers grieving when she let go of her old life. She would have a funeral for the death of her old ideas. The memory and sincerity of the demise has had a profound effect on her life today. When she tries to dig up the bones from the past, she is reminded that she does not have to go there anymore.

She opened her eyes and heart to the love and happiness that God wants for her. She has come to believe that she deserves to be happy and that she has earned the right to insist upon enjoying life.

She does not suffer very well and has had enough hurt and pain. Her faith is stronger because of her life experiences; life is not an endurance contest anymore. She lives by inspiration and not by desperation.

She gave up fighting, especially with herself. Her insecurities that manifested her many fears have been removed. She has had many revelations of the mysteries that very few have experienced. When she thought that she was being patient, she was really being tolerant. She was so in control that she was out of control. She thanks God for keeping her safe when she was walking on fire.

Her success in real estate was determined by how well she controlled her clients. She suffocated spiritually until she realized that freedom came with letting go and not hanging on. She had to step aside and see what God had on the agenda.

She is the happiest when she is not tripping over herself. She continuously exercises her spiritual muscle and keeps her eyes open. The more she thinks that she knows, the more she realizes how little she really knows. She has sought answers when there was none. She has learned that it does not matter what others believe or practice; they are still one in the same.

She has had the privilege of meeting people from the bazaar to the most pure.

She has learned to listen and listened to learn. Most importantly, she has learned to listen to what she is saying and how she speaks. Pretty words can be meaningless unless she wants to hear the sound of her own voice. She has very little to say today. She has talked the disease to death. She listens for what is not being said.

It is a spiritual experience when she peeks into her soul in search of the honest to God truth. It was necessary for her to make the discoveries before she could recover. She had to name what was blocking her from the sunlight so she could claim and change.

Behind every spiritual step, there is an action. She found honesty to intense at times. She was told that there would be no gain without pain and that pain is optional. Either way, she knew that she had to face and embrace the truth.

For many years when she was unable to say, no. She was driven to help others. She felt responsible to give back what she had been given. There were times that she would sacrifice to help others. She looked for birds with broken wings. She hid behind others so that she did not have to look inside at herself. She would breathe strength and hope into broken souls. When she saw the lights going on, she knew that God was alive and well. It was reassuring to see that the miracles never stop and God is still watching over His kids.

When serious problems surfaced she did not have anything to draw from, she had given it all away and did not save enough for herself. She had stopped working her program because she was to busy helping others. She was told not to sponsoring for five years. When she moved to Colorado, it was a huge relief to fill up her cup and heal.

The old timers need a personal support system and at times more then the newcomers. It is assumed that if we have not had a drink for years, we are cured. Wrong, the further away we are from our last drink, the closers we can be to the drink. We have to stay green and maintain the habits of sobriety. We have only a daily reprieve from the disease.

There are times when she thinks it would be nice to have a glass of wine. She has to remember what the drink did to her and to stop romancing the idea. Even now, she has to think the drink through when it starts to talk to her. She drank for effect not because it tasted good.

She has had dreams that she got drunk and did not want anyone to know; thank God, they were only dreams. Whenever possible she avoids being around people who drink. If there is a situation that she has to attend where alcohol is served, she makes a point of having plan "B" so she can leave if she gets uncomfortable. Most of her friends know and respect that she does not drink and have soft drinks for her. On special occasions her friends have bought non-alcoholic champagne. She has had to refuse their kindness; it is too close to the real thing.

When she thought that she had resolved all of her issues, another defect or destructive pattern would surface. She had a problem with retail therapy; she messed up her credit and had to cut up her cards. She had to pay cash for years before she could be reinstated. She has learned to manage better with a list of needs.

She got some not-to-friendly letters from the IRS. It took her five years to pay them back. It seemed strange when the letters stopped after she paid off her debt...

She has made financial amends to everyone that she has owed. She learned a valuable lesson in financial responsibility. It hurt when she saw something in a store she liked and knew that she could not afford to buy it. She felt bad when she could not afford to buy for her kids and grandkids. She had to say no a lot when she was invited to go or do something with friends because she was broke. She was grateful for her needs being taken care of.

All of the penny-pinching has helped her prepare for living on a fixed income. She has learned that less is okay and does not feel deprived.

She has made peace with the men who were in her life. She has learned to be a friend with some special men and women. She has learned to halt when she gets, hungry angry lonely or tired. There are times when she is concerned about being too complacent and comfortable.

She listens for the message and not to the messenger. She has had the privilege of attending one of the world's greatest classrooms. The 12-steps give spiritual direction to her life.

There are fallacies and misconceptions that have polluted the program. We are earnest about refraining from any opinions in regards to outside issues. We embrace all of God's Kid's, regardless of what they have done or where they come from.

We go to meetings and more meetings. We are very fortunate in California to have about 400 meetings a week in our area. It is possible to sit in a meeting from 7:00 a.m. to midnight. The hand of AA is always out day or night.

There is no other love greater than what one alcoholic has for another. We understand because we have been there and did that.

She went to AA to save her ass and not her face. It is not about looking or being good. It does not matter if they come from jail or Yale; we are all drunks who are just one drink away from insanity, prison or death...

She had to change her habits and take different routes

away from the liquor store. One thing in AA that is constant is change. She wanted to understand and intellectualize the program. She put up a good fight before she surrendered. She knew that there was no other place for her to go. She has grieved with each letting go and was told that she had to let go absolutely.

She discovered that it is impossible to be miserable and grateful at the same time. She has had days when all she could do was thank God for one more day sober.

She wasted hours processing something that she did not understand before she could accept the truth. Her thinking was so twisted and her emotions so deceiving. Much of what she thought she believed turned out to be the opposite.

Looking good was no longer important. She had to give up the disguise that she had hidden behind and become venerable. She had to die to the old, so she could be born again.

She learned humility from a man who had lived in the weeds. She learned about honesty from an ex-con and acceptance from a former prostitute. She learned about God from a lesbian. They are all God's prodigal kids, who like herself were given a second life.

Thank God, for being forgiving and for helping her to forgive herself. God's Kid does not point fingers or judge. It is not our job to figure out God. What is important is that we, keep walking, talking and believing, no matter what.

She once thought that God was someone that she needed to see, feel or touch. She learned that our actions do speak louder than our words.

She question God and doubted that she was deserving of happiness and sabotaged her sobriety. She tried to manipulate God into doing it her way, selfishly wanting to collect. She did her penance and wanted God to reward her. She wanted instant relief and spiritual gratification.

She was being spiritually prideful and self-righteous. Little did she know that she had already been rewarded, she just did not realize it?

She had to keep letting go completely or it was going to kill her. She had to let go of control and learned that letting go was easier than trying to hang on. Surrender to win was a spiritual principal that she had to learn.

It has been a long process of sorting out the mess from the message and learning to live in the solution and not the problem. She wanted to get well fast. She discovered that it was impossible for her to emotionally recovery without having a solid spiritual foundation. Sometimes God does not always have all of the answers.

The longer that she walks the walk, the easier it is for her to side step the land mines. She relies on guidance and intervention when she has to make a major decision. She has fought, cussed and fired her God and knows that He/She is smiling. She is no longer an escape artist.

When her head and heart are in conflict, she stands still. When she gets affirmation, she can move forward knowing that she is not alone. Ultimately, the results are none of her business.

She can see and feel situations in a very different way. At times reality can be shocking when the illusions are gone. She did a lot of walking across freeways and ignored the traffic, only to be continuously run over. She was bruised, cut and bleeding before she realized the insanity of doing the same thing expecting different results. She was having crises, creating crises or looking for someone in crises. Thank God, she ran out of band-aids.

She does not want to walk behind or ahead of anyone; we walk together hand in hand. What we say or do can have a profound effect on another person's life. When it comes her time to transcend out of this body, she wants to leave more behind than what she has taken.

*****

However, my hair is turning gray and my skin no longer fits
On the inside, I am the same old me
I have learned that life goes on and will be better tomorrow
I have learned that regardless of your relationship with your parents,
You will miss them when they are gone.
I have learned that making a "living" is not the same as making a "life."
I have learned that life sometimes gives you a second chance.
I have learned that you should not go through life with a catcher's mitt on both hands.
You need to be able to throw something back.
I have learned to make decisions with an open heart,
I have learned that even when I have pains, I do not have to be one.
I have learned to reach out and touch someone.
I have learned that people will forget what you said; people may forget what you did,
People will not forget how you made them feel.
I have learned that I still have a lot to learn.
Author Unknown

*****

Thank-you for "Walking the Walk" with me
Barbara

NOTES FROM GOD'S KID'S

Only what we give away enriches us from day to day.
For not in getting but in giving is found the lasting joy of living.
Helen Steiner Rice

Thank-you so much for the gift and blessings of your book! Reading it has helped me to hang on and not give up on Him, my faith or my hope. I will be sure to pass your book along. My love and prayers always. "One of His many Children"

Only GOD knows where you get the words and thoughts that fill your book. It is a gift that few are given and fewer give to those who choose to use those words and thoughts to enlighten themselves and those around them. Thank-you for sharing this wisdom and wit with me. I look forward for more. .Al

Enclosed is a check for the replacement of your rear light on your car. Thank you so much for being so calm and reasonable. I very much look forward to reading your book. You are clearly an unusual woman. Hope your Easter is filled with blessings. You've already been a blessing to me. Pat

You have been a very special friend and neighbor. We have shared many common interests, the beach and our Shih-tzu's Joey and Moses. I look forward to helping you with your proofing and wish you success in reaching the hearts of your readers. Joane

God has plans for you. There are a lot of new comers who still need your experience, strength and hope. (Lots of old comers too). God bless. Your friend,. Bob$

God really blessed my life when He made it possible for our paths to cross. I am so grateful! Love Clairene

Your albums really rocked me back. I'd been thinking about my lack of photos for about a week and half before your bombshell arrived. WOW!! You were my first wife and like my first born will always occupy a special place in my heart and soul. I am so grateful to have the pictures (I had none). Ex-husband Mike

Thanks so much for a great evening. I was proud to help give you your sobriety cake but most of all to meet your beautiful daughters. I found them charming and so much fun. Thanks again, Joanne

Thank-you so much for sending "Rosie" to us. We absolutely love her! She is adorable and full of personality. She is a wonderful addition to our family...Doctor Kenny and Lynn and family

I've been thinking about you for the past couple days. I wanted to say thank-you" for opening your home to me. When I think about it, I am surprised that there are still kind and loving people like yourself. Especially when I, am into my own needs. ..Yolanda

Thanks for all your support and caring in August. It was without a doubt the worst month of my life. But your help eased the pain. This Christmas will not be as bright without Mom but I know there's a new star in heaven. ..Doctor Pal

You've always been a good friend. Thanks for being there when I've needed you.... Love Pat

God bless you and thanks for being a part of my recovery. You were so helpful after my mom died. I thank you for listening. If you don't remember it was over a year ago last December. Thanks again for your sobriety. You are truly a gracious gift from God...Dennis

My God you were wonderful to me. Thank-you so much for your help and support and the rides home too.... Joyce

Amazing isn't it, we come to find out how not to drink and are given the most precious gifts. Life long friends. ..Love Rose

Thank you for being in my life. Thank you for sharing so much knowledge and beauty about sobriety and life. Most of all I thank you for teaching me how to love God as I understand him. You have been a gift from God. My life has changed so much. I feel at peace with others, especially my family and me. ..Your friend Lucy

Of all the gifts that life can send. There's none more special than a friend. This card says it all. I feel you are one of the gifts I was given this summer. ..Jody

I think that a gift from God that comes to me through you. Thank-you for being my friend...I love you my dear best friend! You are going to be deeply missed. .. All my love, Sher

Thank you for opening your home to a bunch of us in recovery, such good people, good food and good sharing. I always enjoyed seeing what you've done with that steal of a deal home of yours, it's darling.… Thanks, Ginny

I want to thank you for diving to Denver to celebrate my birthday. Also for the beautiful medallion. What a treasure!!. I will wear it with pride. Also, I want you to know what a beautiful and powerful example your recovery is to me. Your commitment to God first and your sincere love for this AA program really touches my heart and inspires me to continue trudging the road to happy destiny. ..Love Alice

What can I say but Thank-you?. I'm finding peace inside me. I walk with my God. Your a very special Lady "my friend always". ..Jeannie

Thank you because you care…we are what we are today. Half Measures

It takes all kinds of people to make a world. What a nice world it would be if there were more people like you.… Geneva

Words can't tell you how much you have helped me change my life.… Bonnie

Thank you so much for your kindness and generosity in allowing us to stay in your home. We were very comfortable and we appreciated it very much. Thank you.… Mike and Sandy

I just want to thank you from the bottom of my heart for opening up your beautiful home to my best friend Susan and for being such a fabulous tour guide and friend. YOU ARE A MIRACLE!! I am grateful for your concern for me and my family and all that you have shared. God Bless you and your ministry with your girls. Thanks again.…. . Lisa

Your thoughtfulness as ever was absolute perfection. Thank you! You are a very special lady.… Sandy

Regardless of what happens, Nancy and I love you already. You've been a real blessing! You are proof that we can entertain angels if we align ourselves to God and try to be of service.… Love you Jerry and Nancy

Do you realize we met when Brandis was 5 years old? Do you remember how I always said you came to Colorado (sent by God) for me? Well I'm sure from your point of view you can look back and see much more! And now I do too. God used you so much and I'm eternally grateful my dear friend! Here's my new view and I'm so blown away when I think about it! Besides whatever reasons for you, you came to Colorado. Do you realize God also used you to find the family for baby Savannah 12 years later. Can you imagine? I'm speechless! Maybe you already knew all this but every time I think about it now I get "God goose bumps"- you were sent by God to Colorado for my grandbaby before she was ever conceived. God is Great!! Wow. Thank you for being a willing vessel for God to use!! I love you dearly and miss you terribly. You are constantly in my prayers.. Sher

You set a great example for women in the program. I am so grateful that our paths continue to cross. Thanks for showing up for us all.… Linda M

Thank you for opening your home and heart for a wonderful Thanksgiving dinner!! I have much to thank my Higher

Power for, especially friends like you. I had a great time.... Love
Paula

Just a note to say I love you and I see the love in you. I am wonderful. I had a difficult time for several months when my spouse
made his transition. Prayer is wonderful. I was led to write to
you now..... Love always, Sharon

Being able to share the miracle of sobriety with you—along with
our experiences, strength and hope will always mean a great deal
to me. You dwell in my heart rent-free.... Glenda Mae

God sure works through you. You give so much, what I'm try to
say is, I love you and miss and practice your kindness and loving
words and caring always for this alcoholic and friend. God bless
you and keep you always. Thank you for guiding me and giving
me a God so beautiful.... Love Me

I am so glad that we have gotten to know each other after so
many years of being separated by career's, marriages, and moves.
With each of us going our separate ways we did not have an opportunity to get to know each other as adults. The last few years
that we have been able to spend together have been very special.
We have finally been able to get to know and appreciate each
other. "I am happy to have a sister like you." Love Wanda

Son Joel
Dear Mom, I have so many things I feel for you. Things that
make me happy, things that make me mad, things that make me
glad, things that make me sad. But the things I feel the most is
loved by you. Love

Dear Mom, I apologize for not remembering to send you a card on your birthday. Please find it in your heart to forgive me. I know the card is late but it is still filled with love.

Thanks for always making me feel so special. Love
This card expresses my feelings probably the best. I know you love me and have always tried your best. I want you to know I appreciate all that you have done and I also want you to know I love you.

This card expresses my feelings. I am grateful for your support. Love
With love and happiness today and always. Love
I owe you a dinner, have a happy day. Love

Daughter, Jan

I enjoyed our visit very much. I truly felt nice although I would have liked to be able to have more time. I love you Mom and the time that was spent I will treasure. Always know I am thinking of you. Love

Thank you for your kindness you have given to me and also the time you have taken. I truly enjoyed myself due to all you have done. A memory that will not be forgotten, thanks to you Mom. I love you.

It is a day after mother's day and I am thinking of you and would like for you to know I love you today and always. I would like to be able to have more time to spend with you. The time we can spend I enjoy very much and I look forward to doing your hair too. I love you xoxoxo

I love you Mom and I thank you for listening at times when I need to talk and let things out. You are not only my Mom but also my friend. Thank-you. I love you.

Its truly been wonderful having you close by and to be able to spend this birthday with you. It sure has been awhile since we were able to make you a cake. I would like you to know I am thinking of you a lot. of love.

I really do know how you must be feeling. I hope you have room in your heart for understanding, forgiveness and acceptance be-cause you are loved and never completely forgotten. You mean a very lot to me and although I may not like all the things you do or say, you are accepted. I am glad that you are my Mom, you have taught me a lot and helped me look at the light. Remember I am an individual and to be treated that way. I love you and hope you accept my gift of love.

Daughter, Susan

Mom this card is special just for you. I thought about you and our conversation on the phone and have realized I have a pretty great Mom. The time spent with you was great! The warmth and love that I felt from you was real, there has only been a few times that I felt this way. Mom it took you awhile to find happi-ness but you found it within you. Got to be proud of yourself., Thank you so much for the effort, time and energy given to me by showing us Colorado. The experience is unforgettable. Mom you looked so happy and adorable when you were rafting. A little excitement can do us all good. I love you and will speak to you soon. Thanks again for all you have done. Love

From your daughter who appreciates your generosity, kindness and caring. Let's make a deal, I'll make a strong effort to accept you for who you are in exchange back in return. I love you very much. You know you are my only mother and I am your only wonderful beautiful third child and you can only have just one of those. Love Always

Received your letter with picture. Thanks for thinking of us. What made you decide to have your picture done? You look great! The family is doing well trying to adjust to me working as well as I am able to. Boy, how did you ever do it with four kids? I hope you're doing well health wise and mentally. I hope you find work soon, if you have to you can move here. I will help you get a job at the hospital. We're thinking of you. Peace, love, happiness. Love you

This card is perfect for you! Lately I feel more cared for then I have in years, thanks Mom for your support and motherly talks. It has helped me a great deal. How would I have done it alone? This is what love is and feels like, thank-you, I appreciate all you have done but mostly your warmth and love. Take care, stay warm and healthy. Love you

Hi Mom, thinking about you on this special day even though I won't be with you, you'll be in my thoughts and heart. I miss you and love you and I hope you get feeling better, take it easy. Have a nice day, love and kisses.

Daughter Becky

Mom, I feel that as I crawl, walk and even run through life, I can see that I have gone through many changes and stages. That is where my understanding comes in about you and me. We are very similar in many ways. You are a very beautiful woman and Mom. I see how you must have struggled in many ways. I see myself struggling but I find some strength in knowing that you made it. You give me hope, Mom. I love you Mom and thank God that you are my mother. It brings tears to my eyes thinking of all the times that I have wasted by not letting you into my heart. My being so petty when I could have enjoyed having you in my life. I use to wish that I had a curtain type of Mom and even felt like I never had one, but really, you are a perfect Mom for me. God is a very wise God. I know Mom that you have been there for me and I feel comfort in knowing that you will always be there, even when I am not the most lovable daughter. I see that you have become so understanding, kind and gentle, not only with me but with my children. Love your baby Girl Rebecca

Notes from Grandchildren

Sorry this is probably late. I hope that you have a wonderful birthday with your family. I also wish you all the love and happiness in the world. In this card I send you joy, love, memories and a piece of my heart because you will always have that special place their Grandma. Thank you for everything, support, hope, joy, fond memories and above all love. It is always nice to know someone is there for you 100% and I know that I have that in you, thank you. Adrienne

Thank you for letting me stay with you and taking care of me. I really appreciate your being there for me. I'm glad I got to know you better and got to spend time with you. I'll miss you at graduation but I understand. I wish all the luck in the world on your return to California and new life. I love you!.... Adrienne

Dear Grandma, how are you? I am fine. I just adore your card. It's very pretty. I am sending you a birdie I made by just folding paper. I didn't make it from instructions. I am going to buy something very special with my money. I am very sorry I haven't been writing you but I am busy with school and stuff. I got 5-A's and I-B on my report card so you can see I am doing real well. Dear Grand-ma, Thank you very much for the pretty card and money. I am going to California soon. How do you like your new house? I am going to have a Birthday Party and Mom is taking me to Fun Time USA. And I am going to Wet Willis has water slides. Love always, Adrienne

Dear Grand-ma, How are you? I am fine. I really liked the bracelet you sent me. I put the charm on my necklace so I can think of you when I see it. I am doing very well in school. I hope you think that is good. Because it is hard to write in your best handwriting. I think you have pretty handwriting. I love you. Adrienne

Dear Grand-ma. Thanks for the dollars. I bought some pretty cool stuff. I had a good Christmas and a good winter vacation. Maybe someday I will visit you. Love your grandson, Jared

Dear Grandma. Thanks for the money. I used it for buying a spy-teck. It alerts me when someone comes by. Is it snowing over there? I got an air hockey for Christmas. Love Zachary (January I-I991)

To Grandma from Jared, Zachary, Brian. Dear Grandma, thank you for the dollars. To buy myself a toy. Zachary bought a watch for himself. He likes it very much. It cost four dollars. It can change different wrist. Love Jared, Zachary and Brian

(December 1993) To Grandma. How are you doing? I miss you so bad. My teacher is nice. Her name is Miss Shubie and second in my class. I love you so bad. From Chantal

Grandma I could not thank you enough for the gift you have given me and all the support you've shown and showered me with. Although this card isn't as much as a sacrifice as the cash you gave me, the same amount of love went into it. Love Zack

✵✵✵✵✵

Once upon a time, there was a child ready to be born. The child asked God, "They tell me that you are sending me to earth tomorrow, how am I going to live there being so small and helpless?"

"God replied, "Among the angels, I've chosen one for you. Your angel will be waiting for you and will take care of you."

The child asked, "Tell me, here in heaven I don't have to do anything but sing, smile and be happy."

God said, "Your angel will sing for you and will also smile for you everyday. And you will feel your angel's love and be very happy."

The child asked, again, "How am I going to be able to understand when people talk to me if I don't know any language?"

God said, "Your angel will teach you the most beautiful and sweet words you will ever hear, with much patience and care, your angel will teach you how to speak."

"What am I going to do when I want to talk with you?"

God said, "Your angel will place your hands together and will teach you how to pray."

"I've heard that on earth there are bad people, who will protect me?"

God said, "Your angel will defend you even if it means risking its life."

I will be sad because I will not see you anymore.

God said, "Your angel will talk to you about me and will teach you the way to come back to me, even though I will always be next to you."

Now there was much peace in heaven, but voices from earth could be heard and the child hurriedly asked, "God, if I am to leave now, please tell me my angel's name.

*God said, her name in not important, you will simply call her "**Grand-ma**."*

Author Unknown